LEADERSHIP
INSIGHT

LEADERSHIP INSIGHT

KEYS TO INCREASE
YOUR INFLUENCE
AND MAKE A
DIFFERENCE

FAITH BIBLE COLLEGE INTERNATIONAL

AVAIL

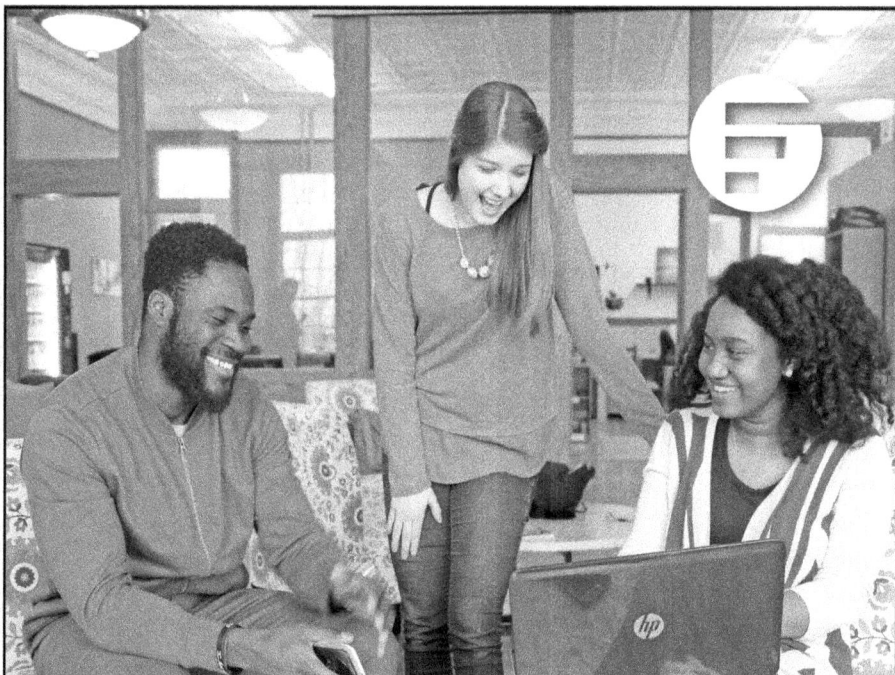

DAY 1 — DEBT-FREE

MISSION STATEMENT

The mission of Faith Bible College International is to prepare professional, Pentecostal Servant-Leaders who make a world of difference in fulfilling the Great Commission of the Lord Jesus Christ.

CONTACT US!

Faith Bible College International

29 Main Road | Charleston, ME 04422

207-285-3373

www.faithbci.org

Follow us @faith_bci

VISION

FBCI is a single focus institution of higher learning, instructing men and women in theological studies while preparing them to be pastors, evangelists, missionaries, educators, worship leaders, and more. In adhering to our mission, we champion our students to discover, develop, and fulfill their purpose in the Christian ministry. Through inspired classes, anointed chapels, individual mentoring, and hands-on ministry experiences, the students will mature in their giftings. Furthermore, we endeavor to offer students a path to the blessing of ministry without the burden of debt.

FOREWORD

There is a word found nowhere in the Bible (at least not in the King James Version and only a handful of times in other primary versions), yet that word is used almost daily in most Christian organizations. A web search of this word will give you enough reading for years to come.

Most organizations' angst revolves around the lack of this word, and those that flourish value it in all its manifestations.

The word is *Leadership*.

Ask ten random people about their understanding of leadership, and you will get as many answers. None of them would be wrong. All of them would be right. But, you will gravitate toward the one that fits your current context.

Hence, *Leadership Insight*.

My friend Dr. Matthew Ward, President of Faith Bible College International, has assembled a diverse group of voices to share their understanding of and perspectives on leadership in their areas of expertise.

In this book, you will find golden nuggets that provoke and awaken thoughts that lead you to your own chapter on leadership.

I think it would be amazing if—after you've read this book, highlighted what spoke to you, and written notes in the columns—you would write its next chapter . . . something like Acts 29 where the book of Acts is continuing through you.

What would your chapter on leadership deal with? What would be your core message as you empower and develop other leaders? Most importantly, how would you describe your leadership—substance and style—and your motivations as a leader?

If you respond to the paragraph immediately above, the mission of this book will be accomplished.

Stay strong, and keep leading!

—Sam Chand
A friend of Dr. Matthew Ward and FBCI

CONTENTS

INTRODUCTION

Who would have thought that one's first leadership lessons could be learned from Disney's *Peter Pan*! Whether you saw the movie or not, surely you sang Ted Sears and Winston Hibler's lyrics to "Following the Leader," or you actually followed the one who knew the song. While leadership manifests itself differently in its myriad of arenas, it encompasses the traits described by Rutgers Business School distinguished professor and Institute for Ethical Leadership director—Dr. Joanne B. Ciulla. She states:

Leadership is not a person or a position. It is a complex moral relationship between people based on trust, obligation, commitment, emotion, and a shared vision of the good.

Leadership Insight expounds on that relationship using the voices of men and women actively engaged in nourishing the souls of future leaders as well as those of seasoned veterans on the front lines of the church, business, and the marketplace.

- **Trust:** Follow Pastor Doug Clay, Dr. Courtney McBath, and Timothy M. Hill as they reflect on the importance of integrity, transparency, and collaboration as leaders communicate their messages both in times of crisis and peace.
- **Obligation:** Hear from Dr. Dave Martin, Dr. Matthew M. Ward, and Dr. Chris Bowen as they share the significance of accountability in a person's immediate personal and professional lives as

well as the responsibility to successfully transfer one's leadership mantle to future generations.

- **Commitment:** Join Lisa Potter and Martijn van Tilborgh as they encourage leaders to explore the power of following the Holy Spirit's leading to die to self and embrace new opportunities to fulfill God's vision and further the kingdom by any means.
- **Emotion:** Accompany Marcus Mecum, Jim Cymbala, and Dr. Sam Chand as they reveal how one can experience joy and happiness through servant leadership smack dab in the middle of God's will while bearing the burdens of shepherding others from the womb to the tomb.
- **Shared vision of the good:** Learn from Natalie Born and Phil Cooke about how prioritizing the health of the organization and meeting the needs of the team will guarantee success when it comes to waging internal and external leadership wars as well as capitalizing on opportunities.

Regardless of your position or area of influence, be encouraged by the insights of these leaders in their fields as you endeavor to inspire and galvanize—and those who love and admire you follow . . . "Wherever [you] may go!"[1]

---

1 "Following the Leader" by Ted Sears and Winston Hibler, released February 5, 1953, track A4 on *Walt Disney's Peter Pan Soundtrack*, Disneyland, DQ-1206.

LEADERSHIP PRINCIPLES FROM JESUS' LIFE

PASTOR DOUG CLAY

Jesus practiced servant leadership better than anyone. To me, there is no greater demonstration of His commitment to service than when He, the King of kings, was willing to wash the feet of His followers (John 13:1–17). There are many ways to "wash the feet" of those whom you lead. It can be as fundamental as feeling equally or more excited when someone else on your team succeeds than when you are complimented for a job well-done. It's not having to talk so much about yourself but inviting others to talk about themselves. It's having others feel better about themselves when they are around you.

Jesus was willing to invest in people others would have dismissed. Consider the first time Jesus met Simon Peter. In John 1, after they were introduced, Jesus said to Simon, "I'm going to call you Peter." Simon means "small"; Peter means "rock." The Lord was saying, "Peter, you're the kind of person I want to build My church on." By changing that apostle's name from "small" to "rock," Jesus raised Peter's confidence and began building a servant who would become a world changer.

It blows my mind to contemplate Jesus as all-knowing and how that divine knowledge interacts with His love for and relationship with each of us. Jesus knew Peter would deny Him. But Jesus saw Peter from day one for who Peter could be, not just who he was in that moment. It was as if the Lord saw Peter preaching on the Day of Pentecost and operated on that vision rather than on the basis of Peter denying Him.

Jesus modeled trusteeship rather than ownership in His leadership.

Jesus modeled trusteeship rather than ownership in His leadership. People who lead with this mindset regard themselves as trustees of their positions for the good of their respective circles of influence rather than as owners for their own real or symbolic benefit. Regardless of the externals of our positions, as followers of Christ, we are all stewards of the gospel and our calling to connect the lost with that good news and point them to the Savior.

Jesus exercised leadership over life's circumstances. He took what others might perceive as distractions or interruptions and recognized divine appointments. When the woman who had been bleeding for twelve years touched His garment, Jesus stopped to heal her, even though He was headed elsewhere (Mark 5:25–34). Interruptions can lead to divine appointments.

Jesus fed His own spiritual well-being, recognizing that He had to remain in touch with His Father if He was to carry out His Father's plans for ministering to others. Jesus constantly slipped away to spend time with God. I carry a deep burden for the spiritual well-being of our ministers. I was recently talking to a minister who is in our restoration program and asked him how he was doing. He replied, "I've never felt this healthy spiritually!" Although I was excited for him and was encouraged by his comment, I asked myself why he couldn't feel spiritually healthy while in the ministry.

Finally, Jesus finished well, and He had a succession plan. Any questions about whether His ministry was effective or not? It is still at work today in the worldwide body of Christ. The key to that continuity was Jesus' ability to lead even as He was planning to transfer that leadership to others in order to propel His ministry forward. He told the disciples He would not always be with them, but through the power of the Holy Spirit, they could function as His successors (John 16:5-15).

If servant leadership is the umbrella description of Jesus' leadership style, it is also valuable to look at key character traits Jesus lived out to perfection as our model God-follower.

Jesus maintained healthy *spirituality*. His heart belonged completely to His Father. "The eyes of the Lord move to and from throughout the earth that He may strongly support those whose heart is completely His" (2 Chronicles 16:9, NASB). That is the essence of spirituality: complete identification with our heavenly Father.

Integrity is better defined by actions than just words. As it relates to spiritual leadership, integrity is not so much something we do as much as it is who we are. Integrity is all about personal wholeness versus fragmentation. Integrity doesn't involve divided loyalties or interests. Integrity doesn't allow our lips to violate our hearts. Integrity doesn't allow popularity to override principle. Integrity doesn't break promises that are made. Integrity doesn't mean perfection, but it does mean consecration.

Jesus is our model for spirituality. He is our model for integrity.

And, at every point in His life, He is our model for *humility*. It requires unflagging diligence to walk in spiritual confidence while simultaneously nurturing a humble heart. Yet, humility is a spiritual discipline that, when practiced, guarantees that God will show up in a powerful way. "If my people, who are called by my name, will humble themselves and pray and seek my face and turn from their wicked ways, then I will hear from heaven and I will forgive their sin and will heal their land" (2 Chronicles 7:14, NIV). What a promise! I also return regularly to Psalm 25:9 (NIV): "He guides the humble in what is right and teaches them his way."

Why is Christ-like character important? Making Jesus' character your own will impact your ministry in three key ways.

Why is Christ-like character important? Making Jesus' character your own will indelibly impact your ministry.

You need character for the sake of your *reputation*. Ministries that are respected are led by ministers who can be trusted. First Timothy 3:7 (NIV) says, "He must also have a good reputation with outsiders, so that he will not fall into disgrace and into the devil's trap." Nothing will ruin your reputation faster and more permanently than a breach of ethical integrity.

> *"Choose a good reputation over great riches; being held in high esteem is better than silver or gold."*
> —Proverbs 22:1 (NLT)

> *"If you have to choose between a good reputation and great wealth, choose a good reputation."*
> —Proverbs 22:1 (GNT)

You need Jesus' character for the sake of your own *character*. If it is important to keep a good reputation, it's a thousand times more important to safeguard your personal character. A corrupt character spoils your reputation.

> *"Beware of false prophets who come disguised as harmless sheep but are really vicious wolves."*
> —Matthew 7:15 (NLT)

> *"A good tree can't produce bad fruit, and a bad tree can't produce good fruit."*
> —Matthew 7:18 (NLT)

You need to demonstrate Jesus' character for the sake of your *testimony*. Your reputation is what people say about you; your testimony is what your character, your behavior, and your words say about God.

What's communicated when a minister lacks ethical integrity? That person is saying that they don't really believe things like Proverbs 21:3 (NLT):

> *"The Lord is more pleased when we do what is right and just than when we offer him sacrifices."*
> —Proverbs 21:3 (NLT)

> *"The sacrifice of the wicked is an abomination to the Lord: but the prayer of the upright is his delight."*
> —Proverbs 15:8 (KJV)

> *"But you desire honesty from the womb, teaching me wisdom even there."*
> —Psalm 51:6 (NLT)

Jesus' integrity was unimpeachable. Billy Graham once said, "Integrity is the glue that holds our way of life together. We must constantly strive to keep our integrity intact. When wealth is lost, nothing is lost; when health is lost, something is lost; when character is lost, all is lost."

Pastor Doug Clay is the chief executive officer of the General Council of the Assemblies of God. As general superintendent of the Assemblies of God, USA, part of the largest Pentecostal denomination in the world, he is a member of the denomination's executive leadership team and executive presbytery.

THE COMMUNICATION PROCESS

DR. COURTNEY McBATH

Communication is one of the most overused words in our vocabulary, but the act of communication is one of our least consistent practices! We spend a lot of time talking about communicating, but we don't seem to do it very well. It reminds me of Christians who use the words "pray" or "prayer" ten times as often as they actually pray. There's a reason why some terms are used frequently but not practiced consistently, and it's based on the disconnect between the heart and the mind.

In our hearts, we know we need to pray—to communicate with God—but our minds lower the priority of prayer until it becomes something many of us only do when we become desperate. Communication with others tends to follow the same pattern, based on a similar disconnect. Our hearts know very well how important it is to communicate thoughts and actions with others. Our minds . . . not so much.

There's a reason why "communication" is used frequently but not practiced consistently, and it's based on the disconnect between the heart and the mind.

Tim LaHaye once quipped, "Communication is to relationships what blood is to the body!" Somehow our minds lower the need to communicate to a level of priority in which we only do it when absolutely necessary . . . enter crisis. When I faced crisis, my communication skills grew exponentially. I'm not implying that I became a better communicator, but I did start communicating more frequently. The pressure of the crisis forced my mind and its priorities into agreement with what my heart had always known. If we can capture some of the lessons learned and the habits forged during crisis in this critical area of communication, we can improve our efficiency and effectiveness as leaders.

COMMUNICATE IN CONTEXT

Normally, the discussion about communication begins with the message; however, crisis has taught me that my message is not as important as understanding whom my message is for. My message may change, but my target does not. In fact, knowing my audience better may actually adjust my message. So we'll start by discussing the process of determining your audience.

When COVID-19 began, I was immediately concerned about the food-insecure of our communities. In haste, I began to develop a communication strategy that was social media-driven. As I thought about my audience, I realized that this might not be the best strategy. The elderly were more likely to be stuck at home with no food and more susceptible to the long-term negative impact of the coronavirus. My audience wasn't all on social media. Radio, television, personal calls, and written communication might be more effective than social media for them.

When we're leading in crisis, we have a specific problem we are attempting to solve. Our leadership is extremely pragmatic because crisis calls for effective action, not the optics of cool leadership. We immediately start thinking about the best practices for reaching our audience—there is so much at stake. How do we ensure the same commitment to our communication process when there is no crisis?

THE ISSUE MAY NOT BE A CRISIS . . . FOR YOU

Not every issue we set out to solve is a crisis for everyone. It may not be a global crisis. It may not be a pandemic. However, to the person in need, it is a crisis. Once we begin to understand our context and collaborate with others to develop solutions, we must communicate as if lives depend on it . . . because they often do. No matter how life-changing your message, it won't matter if it doesn't reach the ear of the person for whom it's meant. No one wants to waste time barking up the proverbial wrong tree.

Once you begin to establish a sense of urgency, you're in a good place to begin thinking about your message itself. In most cases, there are several layers to the message. We need to research in order to be sure we fully understand the problem we're seeking to address. This will require us to communicate in a series of questions or to conduct surveys. We also need to communicate our heart to serve. Our audience and those we serve need to know our motives and our heart to meet their needs. We must communicate with our collaborative partners and tell the people how to access our solutions. Of course, this is more complicated than is needed for some scenarios, but there is no such thing as overcommunicating!

INTERNAL COMMUNICATION

Believe it or not, the place where communication processes most often break down is internally. We tend to take internal communications for granted, which opens up the door for failed interaction after failed interaction. Here are a few simple assessments you need to make as you develop your communication process:

1) Determine the effectiveness of your regular team or staff meetings.
   - Do meetings happen as consistently as planned?
   - Is there an established, ongoing approach to discussion between meetings?
   - Does everyone feel they have a voice as well as access to decision-makers?
   - Is there effective follow-up on action items?
2) Determine the effectiveness of your digital messaging.
   - How accurate and up-to-date is your website?
   - How accurate and up-to-date is your company's app?
   - Do you have a current strategy in place for the use of social media?
3) Determine your communication effectiveness as the leader.
   - How often do you meet with team members individually?
   - How often do you meet with your team as a whole?
4) Determine the clarity of your organization's mission.
   - How clear and simple is your vision/mission?
   - Does your organization know and understand your vision?

- How much does your mission actually impact your actions/ decisions/events?
- Your willingness to not only answer these questions honestly but also ask your team to weigh in will revolutionize the communication of your organization.

WHO DOES THE TALKING?

Leading in crisis has taught me that, sometimes, the messenger is more important than the message. Interestingly, people often hear the heart of a leader or spokesperson louder than they hear the message. This is why choosing who will speak for you is an important call. There are several factors that go into this decision. The person speaking for your team or organization needs to have a good track record. We've discussed the power of trust and that it is intrinsically tied to change. Leadership is, in most cases, moving people from Point A to Point B. When the communicator has a strong track record, they also gain the trust of your audience much more easily. The right person to speak is not always the person in charge or the most articulate. Look for that positive history. The person who speaks for you must possess an empathy that can be felt by your audience.

Leading in crisis has taught me that, sometimes, the messenger is more important than the message.

Empathy can be defined as the ability to understand and share the feelings of another. Some people have it, and others don't, but empathy can't be taught or given. If you have empathy, you can be taught how to better express it, but you have to possess it in the first place. Whatever your message may be and to whomever it's spoken, empathy is critical. It really is true in almost every case: People don't care how much you know until they know how much you care! Whether the communication is with your staff, the teams collaborating, or the communities you're serving, empathy will be a game changer.

COMMUNICATION IS CRITICAL TO COLLABORATION

Your ability to communicate makes every other part of your efforts that much more powerful. When multiple people, teams, or business entities begin to collaborate, the need to communicate well goes up . . . as well as the risk we take if we fail to communicate. For example, if there is a clear message to share in a collaborative setting, there are at least two independent entities or teams that are involved in sharing that message. There must be strong internal communication. The parties collaborating must ensure that they agree on the message as well as how and when to share it. Additionally, a long-term communication process must be in place so that the message remains intact and the relationship between the collaborative partners remains solvent.

COMMUNICATE TO CREATE

It's unfortunate that some leaders only communicate in order to put people in check, correct them, or share difficult information. For some, a communication strategy is merely something to use when you have bad news to share and you want to minimize the damage. But your voice was designed to strengthen, build up, and create—not to tear down. Let's talk through some ideas that will keep your communications both positive and powerful:

- Always prepare for times of communication. Never speak publicly "off the cuff." When possible, write out your thoughts, organize them, and set a time limit for yourself.
- Always identify what you want your audience to remember after you present. Determine two to three of these takeaways, and make sure you "nail" those points in your address.
- Always be clear on who your audience is before addressing them. My worst presentations happened not because of bad content but because I failed to understand to whom I was talking as I prepared the message.
- Always think about how your words are adding value. There are facts to share, and all facts may not be pleasant; but as a leader, you need to find a way to build up your audience even when the news you have to share is difficult.

Your voice was designed to strengthen, build up, and create—not to tear down.

COMMUNICATE TO CELEBRATE

Leaders communicate internally with staff and teams as well as externally with collaborative partners and the communities they serve. However, we sometimes forget a significant communication responsibility of leaders: vision-casting. It's your responsibility to communicate what the future holds and how your people must prepare for and perform in the next season. Leaders share data from past performance and use it to provide the perspective needed to be effective. At the same time, we can't forget to communicate for the purpose of *celebration*!

In order to inspire the people that make the dream a reality, we must learn to recognize every win—to rejoice over every victory. In crisis, you learn the importance of morale and, by extension, the importance of every acknowledged victory. Your challenges are many, your problems seem insurmountable, and your losses are discouraging. When you achieve a win in the midst of this atmosphere, you have to mention it.

The same can be said for times outside of crisis—remember, it may not be a crisis to you, but it is to someone. The need to celebrate transcends pandemic, war, and natural disaster. In those moments between crises, the effective leader still finds something to celebrate. When you don't reach the goal, celebrate the effort. When sales revenue is less than expected, celebrate the improvements. When someone gives their all and, for reasons outside of their control, it doesn't work out, celebrate their efforts. Every time you do this, you're simultaneously casting vision.

COMMUNICATE VISION AND EXECUTION

Leading in crisis teaches us about what works (and doesn't work) in communication. A one-sided communication that shares vision in an abstract way is good, but without an execution plan, it won't get you very far. On the flip side, if we only talk about how we plan to fund and execute the vision but never touch people's souls, then we won't have the inspiration we need.

In *New Thinking New Future*, Dr. Sam Chand gives us great advice: "Leaders need to be bilingual. They have to communicate in the abstract language of vision, and they have to speak the concrete language of execution."[2] In crisis, people are anxious and petrified about what the future

---

2 Samuel R. Chand, *New Thinking, New Future* (Kensington, PA: Whitaker House, 2019).

holds. If they only hear about the logistics of executing vision, they will lack the inspiration to carry out the vision—even if they agree with it! However, people in crisis need concrete facts as well, so they can face the truth and plan for it. It's all about balancing these two aspects of vision.

This places you as the vision-caster in a somewhat precarious position. You still have the power and the opportunity to get results—if you make the effort to become "bilingual." Think about the vision in your heart, and look at it from two perspectives: "What do I need to share to provide people with understanding, inspiration, and comfort?" and "What do I need to share to give people the facts they need about how we will execute this?" You will, essentially, answer the two most important questions: "Why?" and "How?" If you do this, it will give your people both the inspiration and the information they need to fulfill your great vision.

Dr. Courtney McBath is the senior pastor of Calvary Revival Church in Norfolk, Virginia. He serves as the leader of Calvary Leaders Network, a growing group of leaders who serve the global church and marketplace. He is also vice president of Virginia Bible College in Dumfries, Virginia.

LEADING IN CRISIS

DR. TIMOTHY M. HILL, GENERAL OVERSEER
CHURCH OF GOD (CLEVELAND, TENNESSEE)

In my lifetime, there has probably been nothing that has challenged the church more than the COVID-19 (coronavirus) pandemic. While the year 2020 was perfectly set up to be a year of focus, and many of our churches had developed themes around that idea, for many of those same churches, the focus was quickly knocked off balance as the pandemic impacted our nation and world. For many ministries, instead of thriving, surviving became the order of the day.

AGILITY AND HUMILITY

From a personal standpoint, agility and humility became watchwords for me as I faced the challenges of the pandemic.

First, let me explain what I mean by agility. Since the crisis was evolving so quickly—and with such a drastic impact on the health of our nation, as well as the economic stability of the world—I realized as the leader of the denomination, I had to act quickly and decisively. There was little time to contemplate decisions and come up with grand plans. Instead, I had to rely on my experience to make expedient and informed decisions. When issues are coming at you quickly, there is not much time to sit back and hope that they go away or hope somebody comes up with a solution to solve all your problems. During this crisis, we had to act with speed and agility, and I hope our decisions reflected our concerns and hope for this great church that we call the Church of God.

Just like in all leadership decisions, I realized that leading in crisis was not going to be a one-man show.

But not only did I need to be agile, but our decisions also had to be made in humility. Just like in all leadership decisions, I realized that this was not going to be a one-man show. I did not have all the answers. I had to understand that and have enough humility to admit it publicly.

In a crisis, you have to forget titles. It doesn't matter if your title is general overseer or not. Nobody has all the answers in a situation like this. Humility says, "I need help." Humility says, "I need a resource base and a resource team. I need experts." I realized a long time ago that I am not an expert on too many topics—and I am certainly not an expert on COVID-19.

Realizing my lack of strength in dealing with a global health pandemic, I began to put together a team of medical physicians, legal counsel, and people who could speak to the economic impact of the virus. I assembled a variety of people who could speak into and about this crisis.

Humility played a large part in this process. I had to be willing to say, "I don't have all the answers, and I need help." This helps to accomplish a unified and dynamic purpose. A leader has to lead, but as a leader, he must do his best to bring everyone along in the same direction. That doesn't mean we are all going to agree all the time, but we can agree to disagree and still come together at the end of the day.

TRANSPARENT COMMUNICATION

In times of crisis, it is also critically important to have complete and transparent communication. My philosophy in all things, and especially during this crisis, is to communicate, communicate, and communicate. From the beginning, I stated that I may not always say what you want to hear, but I'm going to be honest, and I'm going to be transparent. If I know an answer or can offer a solution, I'm going to get it to our Church of God family. I also promised to do it quickly. That way, as much as possible, we could all be on the same page, having the same information.

I have found that transparent communication is greatly appreciated. There certainly have been times we could have communicated better. We could have said it more clearly, no doubt. But I think, overall, there has been much gratitude that we at least tried to communicate through every forum and venue and with every means possible.

During the pandemic, I personally participated in some two hundred different livestream/Zoom/YouTube media calls where I have been able to talk with people. I think that it is critical that we have been able to communicate in this manner. Without a doubt, communication has been key, along with transparency, and that was especially true when we had to announce the decision about postponing the General Assembly, the primary convention gathering for the Church of God.

In my ministry, I have never faced a more difficult decision than the one involving the postponement of the 2020 Assembly. I realize that the decision was not just my decision. There were many leaders speaking into that decision. However, I must tell you that I watched grown men cry over the decision, myself included. We knew it was going to be hard to tell a family that there was not going to be a family reunion. Once the decision was made, I felt it was our responsibility to communicate the decision and then talk about all the nuances that were connected it. Again, it was important to be transparent. And in a time of crisis, people have got to hear from their leader, and his or her communication must be upfront and direct.

Military leaders have said that when the bullets are flying, and the grenades are exploding, basically, you have a choice to go with the predetermined battle plan, or you go with the terrain. Because of the circumstances, many times, you have to go with the terrain. Of course, there are those who will argue with that concept. And I'm sure the best of both worlds would be to blend the two together. Do not get me wrong. I know we have to plan, we have to strategize, and there are plans we have to have regardless of the circumstances. But sometimes, especially in the midst of a crisis, we have to run with the terrain that we find ourselves traveling on.

In a time of crisis, people have got to hear from their leader, and his or her communication must be upfront and direct.

COUNTERING MISINFORMATION

During a crisis, leaders also must be quick to counter misinformation. I have always believed that putting out correct and transparent communication as soon as possible is absolutely the best counter to misinformation that so easily gets out there in a time of crisis, simply because, honestly, people are scared, afraid, and just looking for the best information they can get.

Because of the nature of the pandemic, we had never passed this way before, and fear abounded. I understand that, and I don't condemn anyone for their fears. This is a deadly virus. I certainly don't condemn anybody that has different opinions because there are so many ways to look at how to deal with this situation. But as general overseer, I had to tell the truth, put the right information out, and put it out frequently enough to counter misinformation.

While it is important to communicate what we know, we also must be honest in saying what we don't know. To be a leader in crisis, you simply have to say what you know and what you do not know. Your followers will appreciate your honesty.

KEEP THINGS RUNNING

Probably most importantly, during a crisis, you have got to keep things running. The work for the kingdom must go on whether there is a crisis or not. When the international offices had to close because of the pandemic, it would have been one thing if we could have said to everybody when we let them go home that day, "Take a two-and-a-half-month vacation. We'll all get back together soon, and we will find everything as we left it." But we couldn't do it that way because we knew that we had to keep things running. Missionaries still had to have their support. Business and records still had to maintain operations. Local churches still had to produce ministry. And let me just say that I have never been more proud of our Church of God pastors. Many had never thought about going digital with their services. Some had never thought about preaching in any other way besides behind the pulpit on Sunday morning. But they were forced to look at new ways of "doing church." Those pastors knew that if they were to have a ministry when this was over, they had to find new ways to do ministry during the pandemic. The bottom line is that we did not have the luxury of putting everything on hold. We just had to find new ways to do ministry. And our pastors and leaders did just that.

We all had to keep things running. Pastors had to keep ministering to the people in their congregations. Talk about a challenge! How do we do that when members are in the hospital? How do we do ministry when we can't even get close to people? The idea of laying hands on the sick had suddenly taken on a whole new meaning.

So, as we saw the impact of the virus lessen, some churches opened back up, with social distancing and required masking. Again, just trying to keep things running. As I noted earlier, we were out of the office, but we were not out of work, so we had to keep things moving.

ENGAGE

We also must be engaged during times of crisis. We have to stay engaged with one another. Those who will have lost when this thing is in the history books are those who refused to engage. Engage with their community. Engage with one another. And engage with things that are going on besides COVID-19.

Let me give you an example. Although my wife Paula and I had taken a few days to get away, I spent one entire morning on the phone with pastors and leaders of African American churches and with our African American state leaders because, in the midst of the pandemic, there had been other tragic situations that enflamed the spirit of racism in our nation. I only bring that up to say that I chose to be engaged with these leaders to assure them that I was praying for them, that I was with them in the midst of the struggle, and that we were in the battle together. I put out several social media posts about racial strife, taking a strong position that might not have been appreciated by everybody. I bring this up to simply point out that there were other things going on besides COVID-19. We cannot be so focused on one issue that we allow other matters not to be addressed. We must be engaged in all matters impacting those we serve.

There were family and other church issues that were going on before the pandemic crisis started and will continue long after the crisis has passed. So, a leader has to stay engaged on all fronts, not just in the current crisis but in everything that is going on.

A leader has to stay engaged on all fronts, not just in the current crisis but in everything that is going on.

STAY FOCUSED ON THE BIG PICTURE

Regardless of what is happening and the circumstances or crisis we find ourselves in, we have to keep the big picture in mind. So, what comes next? What does the church look like after COVID-19? There was talk about going back to normal. Personally, I am not interested in going back to normal. I want to go to better, whatever better is. I want to see us become the New Testament book of Acts church that we had not yet become. That's what I hope we go to. During the crisis, our churches "left the building," and even though we may get to use our buildings again, I want to see the church outside the four walls of our structures. Yes, it will be different, but I want the "different" to be better than what we had previously.

When I say keep the big picture in mind, I'm asking, are we planning? Do we have a strategy in place at our local churches, in our businesses, in our international offices, for world missions, or wherever? Is there a strategy for going forward? And if there is not, I promise you, we can wait no longer. We must get our strategy ready immediately to move our churches and organizations forward.

When the pandemic was still shutting down most of the country, I walked through Terminal D of the Atlanta airport, the terminal where most Chattanooga flights depart. It was empty. It was like a ghost town, at least at that time. Later that same day, I was in the Dallas-Fort Worth airport. DFW was almost empty as well. I use that example to simply say that it is going to be different. It may eventually get better, but it's going to still be different. Different doesn't mean it's going to be bad. It just means that it is not going to be the same.

We have to have a big-picture mentality. We can't get tunnel vision. We have to see the big picture. When I talk about the big picture, of course, I mean the Great Commission. What does it mean for us as a church to finish the Great Commission? We have not set that challenge aside. We didn't put that command on an off-ramp. We must keep following the commandment of our Lord and Savior, and yet COVID-19 has become a part of how we carry out that commandment.

For example, in 2020, the Church of God participated in the GO Finish 2020 Day. It was a day set aside by different faith groups to emphasize soul-winning. From that concentrated weekend of soul-winning, I received reports of thousands that came to know Jesus. How do you do that when you can't knock on somebody's door and say, "Do you know Jesus?" We found ways, and as a result, thousands came to know the Lord.

OCCASIONALLY, HIT THE "PAUSE" BUTTON

Finally, to not only survive but thrive during a crisis, leaders must learn to hit the pause button. Hear my heart—there is absolutely nothing wrong with hitting the pause button. The pandemic was and continues to be a grueling time for our pastors, laity, parents, children, and everyone else. At some point in time, you have to hit pause. If it is only an hour or just a day, you have got to take a little bit of time and just sit back, breathe deep, get some sleep if you can, work on a home hobby or project or whatever you enjoy, and just allow your mind to rest. It is important to pause, rest, and reflect because when this is all over, we still have ministry to do.

The COVID-19 experience has reminded us of what Jesus did: get alone, pause, and rest.

Whether it is a sabbath or a sabbatical, pastors and lay ministers need rest. That doesn't necessarily mean you have to take three months off at a time, but if you can, that is great. Sometimes it may only be an hour, a day, or maybe even a week. There is a reason God rested on the seventh day. He's our example and our model.

None of us are able to select what we will be known for in the pages of history. I recently told others that I really wasn't looking for COVID-19 to be tied to Tim Hill's work in the history of the Church of God. I was hoping that my history would be connected to more exciting things. But, be that as it may, when history books are written for me, for you, and for all of us, I hope that it is said of us that we were found faithful; we followed the leading of the Lord.

When history books are written for me, for you, and for all of us, I hope that it is said of us that we were found faithful; we followed the leading of the Lord.

One of my favorite things to preach about is the man who carried the cross for Jesus, Simon of Cyrene. When I preach about him, I title my sermon "Lessons from the Unexpected Cross." We can learn numerous lessons from that story:

Lesson #1: Jesus carried the cross first.

First Corinthians 10:13 tells us no temptation has overtaken you but such as is common to man, and that with every temptation, God will provide a way of escape. That verse reminds me that He is always there to carry our load. He understands the burdens that we carry because Jesus carried the cross before Simon did.

Lesson #2: Jesus and Simon carried the cross together.

They worked in tandem. They practiced teamwork, at least for a while, as Jesus and Simon carried the cross together.

Lesson #3: Simon, whether he knew it or not, had been geographically, genetically, and spiritually prepared to carry the cross.

Why Simon? He was in the crowd, but why didn't they pick somebody else? At a glance, they looked at him and knew this man had the muscular strength to handle this kind of a problem. Whether Simon realized it or not, his whole life had prepared him for this moment. And our lifetime has prepared us for the ministry opportunities that we experienced during this pandemic.

Lesson #4: People followed him.

Simon's sons were there. From Bible history, we learn that his sons were Alexander and Rufus. Both showed up later in church history.

These young men were impacted by the behavior of their father. Simon didn't crash and burn during a crisis. He just picked up the cross and modeled behavior that impacted his sons' lives in the future. People are watching you, and they are watching me. I want to model good behavior in a crisis.

Lesson #5: As surely as there was a place for picking up the cross, there was a place for laying it down.

Simon picked up the cross when Jesus could not carry it any longer. He not only carried it along the Via Dolorosa, but he carried it all the way to Golgotha. He took not one foot past it, nor one foot short of the destiny of the cross. There was a designated place to lay this burden down. So, as surely as COVID-19 started, it will end, the church of the Lord Jesus Christ will flourish, and we as leaders will end this journey victoriously.

Dr. Timothy Hill has served in national and international Christian leadership for many years. As general overseer of the Church of God (Cleveland, TN), he serves as presiding bishop for over seven million members of the church in over 180 countries around the world.

OWNING IT: TAKING RESPONSIBILITY FOR YOUR LIFE

DR. DAVE MARTIN

One of the most valuable foundational qualities we can admire in great leaders is their immense willingness to take responsibility for their own lives and their own destinies. All men and women of incredible achievement have understood what you also need to understand: There is only one person responsible for the outcome of your life and the quality of your life. That person is YOU. Do you want to be successful? Do you want to do great things? If so, you are going to have to take responsibility for every facet of your life: your achievements, your productivity, your results, your relationships, your health, your income, your debt, your feelings. Everything!

There is only one person responsible for the outcome of your life and the quality of your life. That person is YOU.

Assuming responsibility for oneself isn't easy. We have been conditioned all our lives to blame external circumstances and every other person around us for the parts of our lives we don't like. In modern America, we start by blaming our genetics, our environment, or the poor job done by our parents. But the blame doesn't stop there. After we grow up and leave home, we continue to blame all our failures and flaws on our spouses, bosses, friends, lack of money, lack of opportunity, lack of education, the influences of the media, the lousy economy, and even our children. We have been conditioned from birth to look everywhere for the root cause of our difficulties except in the most logical, realistic place: ourselves.

You must take responsibility for the outcome of your own life.

The cold, hard truth is that you are living, at this very moment, the results of your past choices and decisions. Just as the present reflects your past choices and decisions, so the future will reflect the choices you make starting today. Nothing else can help you. Nothing else can hinder you. Your life is in your own hands, and your hands alone have the power to shape your destiny.

In accepting total responsibility for yourself, you must give attention to every aspect of life that is important to you. You must give attention to your health because health won't maintain itself on simple genetics. You must give attention to your relationships because your relationships won't survive or grow without sacrifice and purposeful effort. You must give attention to your dreams because most dreams die from lack of nurture. You must give attention to your financial status because nobody else will. You must give attention to and take responsibility for everything that matters, making yourself accountable right now to God and to the high standards you are setting for yourself.

In accepting total responsibility for yourself, you must give attention to every aspect of life that is important to you.

One of the most important aspects of taking responsibility for all the various components of your life will be your own willingness to confront the obstacles, circumstances, people, and personal challenges that lie between you and the goals you have set in each of these areas. There is no victor's crown without a struggle. There is no prize without a fight. There is no overcomer without something to overcome. The challenges of life are the things that make most people quit and become most people's excuses. Great leaders don't make excuses. They accept the responsibility of confronting the challenges in their lives.

Most people want to see change in their lives, change for the better. They want to grow and learn and take the stagnant parts of their lives and revive them. They want to win the battles they have been losing most of their lives. But you cannot change what you're not responsible for. If the fault for your problems lies with someone else, you can't do anything to change those problems. The person with the power to change something is the person with the authority and responsibility to change it. So, if you want change, you have some work to do, just like I do. Before you can even begin doing that work, though, you need to accept responsibility for the thing you want to change and admit to yourself that you, and you alone, can turn this ship around because you, and you alone, steered this ship into its present waters.

Believe me; there are a lot of millionaires out there who had far worse lives than you or I did. Some of them had painful childhoods and terrible parents. Some of them were stymied by physical, mental, or emotional handicaps. Some of them were not gifted with high IQs or with the benefit of quality education. Yet they overcame their obstacles because they realized that the outcome of their lives was in their own hands. In the United States, every person has an equal opportunity to make his life better than it is, but nobody can make his life better if he isn't willing to take responsibility for his life. No other changes can possibly occur in you or your circumstances until you are willing to own up to your own responsibility to yourself and become a participant in your own rescue by taking ownership of your own destiny.

You created the present, and you can create the future.

When you accept the premise that there is nothing you can do about your plight in life, you become chained to the life you have. You become a prisoner to your circumstances. But your deliverance from all your limitations begins when you admit that you are responsible for where you are and that you are the only person who can do what it takes to get out of where you are. Your life can begin to turn around when you realize your choices and decisions put you in your current situation; therefore, your choices and decisions can turn things around as well.

If you have been through bankruptcy, for instance, your choices and decisions put you there. If you have been through a divorce or a business failure, your choices and decisions put you there. Of course, there were some outside influences that added to the demise, and, of course, other people played a role in the failure. But you are primarily the person that you are, standing in the place where you are standing because you made the decisions that formed you and your present circumstances. Take responsibility because the rest of this chapter will be utterly useless to you if you are convinced that there's nothing you can do about your life and the direction you are heading. You created the present, and you can create the future.

You created the present, and you can create the future.

Perhaps you're thinking, *But Dave, you don't understand. You don't know what I've been through. You don't understand what people have done to me.* Don't tell it to me. Tell it to Helen Keller, a blind and deaf mute who became one of America's greatest writers and political activists. Tell it to George Washington Carver, a slave who became one of our nation's greatest scientists, educators, and inventors. Tell it to all the men who returned home after World War II to build factories, businesses, schools, and churches. Tell it to the Founding Fathers and early immigrants, who got off boats with nothing more than the clothes on their backs yet carved a nation out of the rugged wilderness. You also can tell it to Abraham, Moses, Gideon, Jeremiah, and other great men of God who were called from humble origins to do great things despite seemingly insurmountable obstacles and resistance. Tell it to any of these people. Go ahead! Whine and complain and detail all your heartaches and disappointments, and see what they say.

If you are like most people, you have all these "reasons" why you cannot be a great leader or do great things with your life, and you have hidden behind these "reasons" for far too long. I want to help you create ways of breaking free from your limitations to achieve all your God-given potential. The battle begins in your mind with the things you are telling yourself right now. The biggest obstacle to becoming a great leader is one's own unwillingness to realistically confront their future. They believe that their future lives will be controlled by the government, by big business, by economic factors, by secretive groups of powerful people, or by sheer "luck." But they don't believe that their futures will be controlled by their own choices and behaviors.

Your future is controlled by you and you alone, regardless of the shifting winds of change that are blowing all around you and regardless of what Washington or City Hall or any other entity is doing.

There is a popular automobile commercial that talks about the two different kinds of people on the road: drivers and passengers. In the commercial, the drivers are having fun and living their lives with passion, but the passengers are just going along for the ride and aren't having very much fun at all.

On the road of life, there also are two kinds of people: drivers and passengers. While the passengers just go along for the ride, accepting whatever happens as their "fate" in life, drivers take responsibility for the direction of their own lives. They grab hold of the steering wheel and guide their lives in the direction they want to travel by maintaining control, making decisions, calling the shots, and determining the pathways their lives will take. Whenever they make a wrong turn, they accept responsibility and get back on track. They refuse to relinquish the outcome of their journey to some unseen person or some unknown force. They want the wheel.

Tim is a great real-life example of somebody who learned this principle in time to avoid disaster and turn his life around. In fact, I'd say that Tim turned his life around 180 degrees because he finally woke up to the fact that he had to take complete personal responsibility for everything that had occurred in his life in the past and everything that would occur in the future.

Tim grew up in a middle-class home with five brothers and a sister. When Tim was eleven, his father was killed in a terrible automobile accident. Tim quickly found life's deck stacked against him. Like so many young boys, he struggled through high school and college, but then, as an adult, he finally had the personal freedom to act upon the fear, anger, guilt, and other pent-up emotions that had brewed within him because of his father's death. So, Tim started living in the "fast lane" and supporting his lifestyle by selling drugs. Eventually, Tim was arrested, convicted, and imprisoned for the behaviors he had chosen for himself.

In prison, Tim had a "pivot point" moment. He woke up and came to his senses, realizing that he was pretty messed up and that he had nobody to blame but himself. Yes, life had dealt him a terrible blow, but life had dealt worse hands to other people who had managed to live happy, productive lives. So, Tim made a conscious decision to change. He knew he alone was the one responsible for his imprisonment, and he knew he was the only person who could turn his life around. He began to work on himself.

For one thing, Tim realized that he had a lot of suppressed anger. He was angry about his father's death and that he had been forced to grow up without a dad. He was angry that the early years of his life had been disrupted and that he had not been able to enjoy the things that other boys his age were privileged to enjoy. He felt sorry for himself and then angry with his father who had died. He was mad at the whole world, which had been so unfair to him, and which seemed unable or unwilling to do anything about his pain. Tim dealt with his anger by turning it inward. He had destroyed his life. He had really messed things up.

When Tim finally put all this together in the solitude of his prison cell, he decided to accept full responsibility for his past failures and, more importantly, for his future potential. He took definitive steps to change things in his life. He read books. He organized prison talent shows where he served as the master of ceremonies. And he started telling jokes because he had a natural talent for humor. Then, upon his release from prison, Tim was fortunate enough to land a great job at a leading talent agency.

Over time, Tim really excelled at his trade. He got noticed not only for his work but also for his talent as an actor and comedian. His performance company even approached Disney with Tim's capabilities, and Disney offered him a role in a major television program. Tim turned down the offer, however, holding out for something that fit him better. Disney made two more offers that he rejected. Tim wanted to take responsibility for the direction of his own life. He had his own idea for a television program, and his idea just didn't match up with Disney's. So, Tim turned down their repeated offers and worked instead to make his own personal dream a reality.

Eventually, Tim was able to star in his own television show, a show he conceived that fit his humor and talent perfectly. The show was about a man who was the host of his own handyman program on television, and this new show became a major hit with the American audience. By now, you have probably guessed that I am talking about Tim Allen, creator and star of the number one television show, *Home Improvement*.

Just thirteen years after his release from jail, Tim Allen was starring in the top television program in America (*Home Improvement*), had the leading role in a major motion picture (*The Santa Clause*), and had the number one book on the *New York Times* Bestseller List (his autobiography, *Don't Stand Too Close to a Naked Man*). I'd call that a turnaround. How about you? And it all began when Tim Allen made the simple decision to accept complete responsibility.

Do you think Tim Allen would have become a successful actor, writer, and comedian if he hadn't accepted responsibility for his own life? Of course not! He would have kept traveling the same worn-out path of repeated self-destructive behaviors that landed him in jail in the first place. He would have continued to be angry and to feel sorry for himself. In prison, Allen was no benefit to himself, his wife, his family, his friends, or society. He would have continued to be a source of pain and trouble for all these people and more, but you can see how dramatically he increased the value of his life to the people around him and to himself by simply owning up to his past decisions and accepting responsibility for his future ones. In a moment of revelation, he went from being a drug pusher to being a future box office millionaire. Not bad for an ex-con!

You are completely and solely responsible for everything you are and everything you become.

You are completely and solely responsible for everything you achieve or fail to achieve. You are where you are and what you are because of yourself, your thoughts, and your behaviors. No one else is responsible or can be responsible for the outcome of your life. I know this may be a harsh dose of reality for some people reading this book, but it's true. A doctor starts the healing process by showing you the cold, hard facts derived from your blood tests and x-rays. Then, facing the objective realities of that truth, he tells you what he can do to help you get back on your feet. In this straightforward chapter, I'm trying to do the same thing. I want to enable you to see yourself and your situation for what they really are. Once you do, I can help you do something about it.

You need to realize that you are doing the work that you chose to do. You are earning the income that you chose to earn. You married the person that you chose to marry. You are living where you chose to live. You have always been free to choose, and you are still free to choose. But in the real world, you must eventually live with the consequences of all the choices you have made or failed to make. You see, the issue here is responsibility, and this issue is one of the most important issues in life. It is rapidly becoming one of the most important issues in society, too, because most of the political bickering that is so prominent in our country right now finds its roots in the two opposing views that people hold on this subject.

What are the two schools of thought on the issue of personal responsibility? On the one hand, there are those who believe that no one is responsible for anything. We are all victims of the external factors and uncontrollable internal powers that dictate our plight. Society, genetics, and the government control individual destiny. Therefore, society and government are responsible for taking care of people and for making many of the decisions that will determine the outcome of their lives. On the other hand, there are those who believe that, in a society, individual responsibility is the most essential element of personal freedom? This group believes that with individual liberty comes individual responsibility and accountability. Therefore, a person is responsible for the consequences of his own choices and behaviors.

Obviously, I fall into this second group, and I believe that the Bible supports this philosophy of the relationship between society and the individual. For a person to be genuinely happy and fulfilled, that person must be legitimately free. But freedom carries with it a necessary measure of personal responsibility. If you are going to make your own choices and plot your own course, then you must live with the consequences, both good and bad, of the choices you make.

Greater progress in your life is possible only to the degree that you accept more responsibility in your life. No one else can or will take up your share of the load. Nevertheless, personal responsibility is a funny thing because the more responsibility you accept, the more often people will be willing to help you. The less responsibility you take for yourself, the less people will want to lend a helping hand.

Personal responsibility is a funny thing because the more responsibility you accept, the more often people will be willing to help you.

The most wonderful reward you will receive for accepting responsibility is the tremendous sense of freedom and satisfaction that it gives you. When you step up to the plate and accept responsibility for your own decisions and for the circumstances you have created in the past and can create in the future, you will feel more positive about yourself and happier with life. You will feel good about yourself and excited about the future. You will feel like you are finally guiding your ship and controlling your destiny. You will feel like you are truly having an impact on your destiny and that you are no longer a victim of more powerful people or unseen forces. So, take responsibility for yourself, and take responsibility for your dreams and ambitions too.

No matter where you might be right now in your life—working for yourself or for someone else—you need to assume 100 percent responsibility for all that falls under your domain. If you don't, you will never really achieve major success, and nothing else will ever really work out for you. So, if you want to be a great leader and create the life of your dreams, you must take responsibility for your life, its direction, and its outcomes. You must give up your excuses, your victim mentality, your reasons why you can't do what you want to do, and all the stories you tell yourself and others to rationalize your current plight.

Someone recently told me, "Dr. Dave, I heard there's going to be a recession and that it's going to be pretty deep and pretty long."

"Well," I responded, "I choose not to participate."

Believe it or not, even the economy and its impact on your life is, to a great extent, a matter of choice. In fact, everything you experience in your life is a matter of choice, whether it is internal or external. You can't always control what other people do and what happens in the world around you, but you can always control how you are going to respond to it. The outcome of your life is the sum of all the responses you make to the various situations that arise.

Moses and Pharaoh are great examples. In the book of Exodus (the second book of the Bible), God chose Moses to be His spokesman and His representative to Pharaoh, king of Egypt. Then God sent Moses to tell Pharaoh to release the Jewish people from their slavery, thus allowing them to travel with Moses to Canaan (the Promised Land). When Pharaoh resisted the demands of Moses, God sent a series of ten terrible plagues upon the nation of Egypt to convince Pharaoh that He meant business and that Pharaoh should comply with His demand. The same ten plagues that built the faith of Moses caused Pharaoh to resist with ever-increasing stubbornness. Both men witnessed the same ten plagues—the plague of gnats, the devastating destruction of horrific hailstorms, the visitation of the angel of death—yet while Moses' heart softened because of that experience, Pharaoh's heart grew more and more rebellious. As someone aptly summarized, "Apparently, the same sun that melts butter hardens clay."

These two men encountered the same God and witnessed the same miracles. But the outcome of their lives and their eternal destinies were radically different because of the different ways they chose to respond to what was happening around them. One took responsibility; the other lived in denial. One chose to learn and grow; the other chose to dig in and resist. One initially resisted but chose to comply; the other initially resisted and increased his level of resistance.

So, God elevated Moses and destroyed Pharaoh on the basis that each man was responsible for his own choices!

Regardless of those things in your life that you cannot control (your family history, your genetic makeup, the economy), you will always have control over three important things. You will always have control over the thoughts you think, the images you visualize, and the actions you take. The choices you make regarding these three ongoing areas of your life will determine the very outcome of your life and the quality of your existence. If you don't like the outcome thus far and the quality is not up to your expectations, you are going to have to change one or more of these three components of self-determination. You are going to have to modify what you think, the way you think, your daily habits, your reading material, your conversation, your dreams and fantasies, or something else because these eventually determine who you are and where you end up.

Wayne Dyer, a well-known author and lecturer, said:

All blame is a waste of time. No matter how much fault you find with another, and regardless of how much you blame him, it will not change you. The only thing blame does is to keep the focus off you when you are looking for external reasons to explain your unhappiness or frustration. You may succeed in making another feel guilty about something by blaming him, but you won't succeed in changing whatever it is about you that is making you unhappy.

You will never become successful if you continue to blame someone else or something else for your plight in life.

The tendency to blame other people and external factors for one's problems reminds me of the elderly man who was lying in a hospital bed, clinging to life, and approaching his final moments. During one of those rare occasions when he was conscious and alert, he noticed his wife of fifty-seven years sitting in the chair beside his bed, and he mustered enough strength to whisper to her.

"Honey," he said, "can you come closer?"

His wife got up from her seat and leaned over his face, placing her ear close to his mouth, so she could hear what his final words might be.

"You know," he said, "you were there with me when the house burned down."

"I know, Sweetheart," she said. "I know."

"And you were there with me when I lost it all, and we had to start over."

"I remember, Darling," she replied.

Finally, he motioned to her to come a little closer. As she leaned even closer into his body so she could discern his words, he said, "You know, Baby Doll, you're bad luck."

Lou Holtz, the former head football coach at six different acclaimed universities, including Notre Dame, said, "The man who complains about the way the ball bounces is likely the one who dropped it."

The circumstances you complain about are typically those circumstances you created for yourself through your thoughts, feelings, and actions, and they typically are circumstances you can change with new thoughts, feelings, and actions. If you really wanted to, you could find a better job, eat healthier food and less of it, go back to school, live in a better house, or be a better mother or father or friend. The problem is you just don't want to. At least, you haven't wanted to until now.

And why is that? Why haven't you done those things that can change the quality and direction of your life? Because change equals risk! If you quit your job, you run the risk of being unemployed. If you try that new venture, you run the risk of being judged by others. If you launch that new business, you run the risk of failing and proving to others that your dreams were just a pipe dream after all. If you make changes in your appearance, you run the risk of losing your friends or evoking their disapproval.

Making life changes is both difficult and uncomfortable. So, if you are like most people, you just settle for the easier path and stay put. Then you complain about your life. Great leaders, however, are people who refuse to accept the status quo. They are people whose ambitions are so strong and whose passions are so consuming, they just have to take the risk. They are men and women who realize their lives are 100 percent the product of their own choices, their own friendships, their own work ethic, and their own ingenuity and determination. Nobody else puts them where they are when their moment of enlightenment comes, and nobody else can get them to the Promised Land. They accept responsibility for themselves and start the lonely journey to excellence . . . the journey to becoming great leaders.

You can do the same if you will begin where they began. You can realize the potential that your Creator has placed within you if you will take responsibility for yourself and then do what's necessary to turn things around. You can begin by taking responsibility for yourself.

Dr. Dave Martin is a coach, pastor, mentor, inspirational speaker, and business leader with a mission to communicate biblical principles of success. Coach Dave is known around the world for his ability to resonate with his audience, providing life-saving insight and wisdom.

NOT MY CIRCUS

DR. MATTHEW M. WARD

BECOME THE RINGMASTER
OF YOUR CIRCUS

The big top. The show. The hippodrome. For children, there are few things more exciting than the circus. An elaborate spectacle of events, exotic animals, sights and sounds that overwhelm the senses, mixed with tangy smells and rich flavors of cotton candy and popcorn, the circus creates an experience unlike any other, and as a small country kid in Bangor, Maine, I loved it when the circus came to town. Each summer, I visited a new world through the transcendent experience of the circus. And at the center of it all was the ringmaster. Conducting. Leading. Orchestrating each transition of the show and capturing the audience's attention.

Through many years of ministry and talking with various pastors on how to best lead their ministries and church communities, I often reflect back to my days as a boy at the circus. From the great Philip Astley to today, the ringmaster conducted the most amazing acts, stunts, and animal tricks. He led the circus with poise and precision. The ringmaster performs in a similar capacity to a pastor serving in ministry. Although the ringmaster stands at the center of the ring for all to see, he plays a specific and essential role within the bigger picture of the circus, but equally as important is *what he is not doing*. Vital work—that the crowd never sees—happens before, during, and after the show. The ringmaster entrusts this work to others who are essential in bringing the circus to life for countless boys and girls.

My goal is to help pastors become firmly grounded in understanding the boundaries that exist in their roles within the larger picture of their ministries and churches, allowing them to see profound improvements in their leadership. God has called leaders to be the ringmasters of their given areas of influence.

God has called leaders to be the ringmasters of their given areas of influence.

THE TENT MASTER

If the ringmaster is in charge of the show's performance, the visible presentation of the circus, who is responsible for bringing the circus together, from the animals to the talent, from the transportation to the tent? Who gives the circus its purpose? **The tent master.**

The tent master, also known as the *boss* or *canvasman*, is in charge of setting up and taking down the circus tent. The dimensions of the tent determine the size of the show. In order for the ringmaster to be successful, the tent master must be in control. The moment the ringmaster starts being the tent master, the circus is bound to fail.

God is the Tent Master over your life.

God has established the dimensions of your ministry and your specific role, your *realm of influence*. It is vitally important we acknowledge that God decides the size of the tent and the realm of your influence within the tent. God has called you to the tent that He designed for you and to the realm of influence that he invites you to fulfill within the tent. Only when you serve within the realm of influence that God has given you can you become the ringmaster of His tent. Your life and your service are important to God. He chooses to use you, but you must be willing to jump into the ring. If you don't, the tent will never go up, and those that God would call by your influence will remain waiting for the circus to come to town.

If you allow God to build the tent, and you step into the center of the ring that He has prepared for you, the Holy Spirit will come alive within you and help you perform beyond what you ever thought possible. God gifted your talents and abilities; He knows how to perfectly build the tent to the right size and shape for your gifts. Invite Him to build the tent around you, step into the light, and watch the circus come alive.

You have more impact than you realize. We all do. Tim Elmore says, "Sociologists tell us the most introverted of people will influence 10,000 others in an average lifetime."[3] Imagine how many people you have knowingly and unknowingly influenced in your life so far. Now, step into God's tent, embrace your realm of influence, and see what He will do with your talents to impact the world around you for His glory.

Each one of us has a realm of influence. The Greek word for this is *metron*. *Metron* is a means of measurement by which God measures the circle of our influence. God has entrusted you with your *metron*. We get into trouble when we start operating outside of our *metron*. Being aware of your *metron* and connecting with the Holy Spirit daily to seek God's guidance will help you walk within the full capacity of your individual *metron*.

---

3 Erin Urban, "Council Post: What Is Your Impact?" *Forbes*, 16 Oct. 2017, https://www.forbes.com/sites/forbescoachescouncil/2017/10/16/what-is-your-impact/?sh=47b8b4196f35.

The apostle Paul addressed the realm of influence that God had placed around him:

We will not boast about things done outside our area of authority.
We will boast only about what has happened within the boundaries
of the work God has given us, which includes our working with you.
We are not reaching beyond these boundaries when we claim
authority over you, as if we had never visited you. For we were the
first to travel all the way to Corinth with the Good News of Christ.
Nor do we boast and claim credit for the work someone else
has done. Instead, we hope that your faith will grow so that
the boundaries of our work among you will be extended.
Then we will be able to go and preach the Good News in other places
far beyond you, where no one else is working. Then there will be no
question of our boasting about work done in someone else's territory.
As the Scriptures say, "If you want to boast, boast only about the LORD.*"*
When people commend themselves, it doesn't count for much.
The important thing is for the Lord to commend them.
—2 Corinthians 10:13-18 (NLT)

Paul acknowledged the boundary placed within the authority he received from God and recognized the importance of the roles of others whom God called to work together to spread the gospel. The relationship of tent master and ringmaster is reflected in Paul's writing. Accepting the boundaries, not boasting of others' work, and not overstepping the boundaries of others allow Paul to thrive within his realm of influence. Paul was careful not to compare his *metron* with anyone else's. Paul demonstrated the mindset of a leader who makes the most of what God has provided through His grace. If Paul were alive today, he might tell us to focus on our circus and celebrate what God is doing with all the people and roles that make our circus special.

The greatest joy in life comes when you step into God's purpose for your life, and you can answer three questions: Who am I? What do I have? And whom is it for? When you understand the answers to these questions, you begin to realize the dimensions of your tent along with the boundary of your role, allowing you to give complete energy, time, attention, and love to those you reach within your realm of influence. The *metron* God has given you is yours only. When we stand before God, you will be accountable for your tent alone.

When we stand before God, you will be accountable for your tent alone.

LET'S GET INTO YOUR TENT

Your tent has boundaries, and your role within the tent has boundaries. Boundaries may range from geographical to certain groups of people. You may have been given a *metron* to reach people who have similar experiences and backgrounds, you may have an unshakeable burden for people in poverty, or you may connect with financially successful people to lead them in a life rich with God's presence, doing His work and finding purpose.

For Charleston Church, our mission is to establish a church in every county within Maine. In addition to Charleston in Penobscot County, over the last few years, God has led us to plant two new churches: one in Hancock County and one in Piscataquis County. We now have churches in three out of sixteen total counties in Maine. According to the Pew Research Center, in 2016, Maine ranked one of the least religious states in the United States. With Alabama and Mississippi coming in first as 77 percent of their polled adults claimed to be "highly religious," Maine ranked 48th with 34 percent of Maine's adults claiming the same.[4] In the area of prayer, Maine ranked 50th with 35 percent saying they pray daily. Only adults in Vermont pray less frequently.

Maine needs Jesus. As I often tell my church family, Maine is God's favorite state! How could God not love a state that produced Joshua Chamberlain and boasts the best-tasting lobster on the planet? Stephen King is still a work in progress. Although Charleston Church generously supports missions all over the world, our primary *metron* is bringing the gospel to Mainers.

Another great example of God's *metron* in action is Faith Bible College International (FBCI), which for the past sixty years has produced professional, Pentecostal, debt-free, servant-ministry leaders. Too many men and women will not realize their ministries due to a lack of training or the presence of overwhelming student debt. FBCI fulfills its unique mission by helping students graduate debt-free, leaning on God's provisions, and being supported by generous, Spirit-led financial partners. By providing strong training and eliminating debt, FBCI sends well-prepared ministry leaders into societies across the world to spread the gospel and love of Jesus Christ.

TWO ESSENTIAL ATTITUDES

Humility and courage are essential attitudes to thriving as the ringmaster of your tent.

Humility will keep you from looking to other tents or expanding your *metron* beyond what God intended. We ought to remain humble and embrace our tents and the unique gifts that our Tent Master has provided. Guard against the subtle poison of arrogance and pride, for

---

4 Michael Lipka and Benjamin Wormald, "How Religious Is Your State?" *Pew Research Center*, 30 May 2020, https://www.pewresearch.org/fact-tank/2016/02/29/how-religious-is-your-state/?state=alabama.

they will take you out of your tent and lead you to places you are not gifted to serve and ultimately to fail. I have seen pastors who succeed within their *metron* but end up looking beyond their realm of influence with great ambition, failing to realize that the success they experienced was due to operating within the boundary of their *metron* in the first place. Led by their personal ambitions, they find themselves no longer in God's tent but in one that they created for themselves and doesn't fit. The ringmaster was never meant to become the Tent Master.

Rabbi Rafael of Barshad told a story that captures the risks of arrogance and pride:

When I get to heaven, they'll ask me, why didn't you learn more Torah? And I'll tell them that I wasn't bright enough. Then they'll ask me, why didn't you do more kind deeds for others? And I'll tell them that I was physically weak. Then they'll ask me, why didn't you give more to charity? And I'll tell them that I didn't have enough money for that. And then they'll ask me: If you were so stupid, weak and poor, why were you so arrogant? And for that I won't have an answer.[5]

We do not always see the entire impact of God's plans for our lives. His dreams are bigger than ours. Yet, we must be careful not to seek the tents of others and miss becoming the ringmaster of the tent God provides. I have seen singers who want to be preachers, pastors who want to be politicians, and business owners who want to be pastors. My advice to them is that success in your own tent is not necessarily God's sign that you are called to take your talents into a different tent. Yes, there are many needs and causes out there, but be careful not to become a bandwagon junkie, carelessly jumping into tents that were not designed for you.

5 Alan E. Morinis, *Everyday Holiness: The Jewish Spiritual Path of Mussar* (Boston, MA: Trumpeter, 2017) 47-48, Kindle edition.

We do not always see the entire impact of God's plans for our lives. His dreams are bigger than ours.

Courage helps you stare the lion in the eyes as you stand in the center of the ring and know that your talents and gifts have prepared you to succeed. Cowardice in the face of adversity, however, will cause you to shrink back from your realm of influence and open the door to doubt. *Am I qualified to do this? Am I too young? Too Old? The last time I tried, I failed.* These doubts and fears shackle a ringmaster. Only courage through faith can quiet all doubts and unleash your gifts for maximum impact.

The Bible contains many stories of courage as an essential attitude to success. In Joshua 1:6 (NLT), "Be strong and courageous, for you are the one who will lead these people to possess all the land I swore to their ancestors I would give them," God encouraged Joshua to have courage within his *metron*. We see David stand up against a giant, stones in hand, amidst the criticisms of his own brothers, having courage through faith, trusting God to provide the talents needed to slay a tyrant. David stayed and fought, saving his nation, and blessing his family as his courage opened the path to kingship. You may face criticism, doubt, and fear in your ministry, but let David be an example of how to act within your *metron*.

My hope for current and future pastors is that they embrace their circus and thrive in their roles as ringmasters. In doing so, they will connect fully with God's plans and *metron* for maximum influence, avoiding the urge to get caught up in the numerous causes that exist. If we join every battle, we risk losing the wars. The Tent Master prepared our tents before we were born. Step into the ring, and experience the power of a Spirit-led, focused life.

Dr. Matthew M. Ward has served as the president of Faith Bible College International since 2015. He has also served as the senior pastor of Charleston Church, one of the largest multigenerational churches in Maine, since 2000.

LEADING A HEALTHY SUCCESSION

DR. CHRISTOPHER BOWEN

S imply by becoming a full-time, founding pastor at the tender age of twenty-four, I could easily write an entire book about the lessons I've learned through ministry. After experiencing twenty-seven years of ups and downs, trials and triumphs, church splits, and building projects and seeing God's miraculous power time after time, I learned the most powerful lesson of all in my life: How to properly let go and release the mantle, along with the pulpit, to a successor.

According to *Webster's Dictionary*, transition is the process or period of changing from one state or condition to another. The Greek philosopher Heraclitus said, "The only constant in life is change." Change is not only essential, it is also inevitable. Change is going to happen whether we like it or not. It is important for us to understand that we must keep up with the moving of the times in order to succeed. This is not a new principle. We have seen it throughout the course of time. In 1903, when the Wright brothers flew the first plane the short distance of 852 feet, a flight lasting a mere 59 seconds, no one ever dreamed of where aviation would be in the 21st century. When Henry Ford rolled out the first Model T automobile in 1908, people never thought the fad would last. Our world is constantly progressing and transitioning. Today, we have a computer, phone, calculator, banking system, map, stereo and dictionary in a device that fits in the palm of our hands. In order for this to become successful, someone had to think outside the box and convince others that it was possible.

Why is it that we resist transition? As parents, we know our children go through developmental changes from infancy to toddlers, from toddlers to adolescents, then to teenagers, then adults. It would be selfish of any parent to want to stifle their child from the transitions necessary to grow into adulthood. As much as we would like for time to stand still, we must realize it never will. We have all said that we wish we could keep them as babies because it's painful to let them go. However, it is essential to allow them to go through the process in order for them to reach their life's purpose.

It is essential to realize that transition is more than just change. It requires willingness to let go of what used to be and grasp hold of what can be in order to grow into something bigger and better. Managing transition requires helping people make the difficult process less painful and stressful. As entrepreneur Leah Busque said, "Life is like monkey bars: you have to let go in order to move forward."

It is essential to realize that transition is more than just change. It requires willingness to let go of what used to be and grasp hold of what can be in order to grow into something bigger and better.

Think of living your life as the driver of a vehicle. It is important to glance in the rearview mirror occasionally to see where you've come from. However, it is crucial to keep your focus on the windshield in front of you in order to reach your destination. Oftentimes, we are so busy looking over the past that we miss our future. As we get older, we tend to resist change. It takes us out of our comfort zone and creates challenges that we are unfamiliar with. We must be willing to adapt to the unknown. Instead of sitting in our rocking chairs complaining about change, we need to embrace the transitions of life.

I learned throughout the last few months of my transition from pastoring that complacency can be very dangerous. Most people experience many mistakes and failures, not when they're taking risks and pushing the boundaries, but when they sit back and relax. The worst thing of all is when you are blinded from the fact because you're the "smartest" person in the room, and you feel that you have made it.

Fortunately for you and me, there's always a room with someone smarter than we are in it. It is so easy to stick to what we know and to our own expertise. Somehow, it seems that we find comfort in surrounding ourselves with people that are further behind us. But what does this achieve? How does that make us grow? How does that challenge us? That would be like hanging out with a class of grade-school students and boasting when we beat them at the game. Well, good for us! We outsmarted them, but what kind of vision have we created in them of us?

There is a lesson to be learned, and this is why I am never the smartest person in the room. I intentionally learn from my college students, my colleagues, my wife, my children, and anyone that I position myself in a room with. This is not about me being the big "I" while you are the little "u" in a certain situation.

I won't achieve this as the smartest person in the room. The only way I will is if I continue to learn, grow, and strive for better. I still catch myself daydreaming at times, and it is true for most of us that our egos continue to fight us day by day. The reason is because we are insecure and scared and become worried that someone may find out that we are not "all that." We become frightened about being average, and we should be if we do not have the right individuals around us! But when you have people in the room with you that are smarter than you and also those who are learning from you, it is a win-win situation! If I am always the smartest one in the room, there is no potential for me to grow, expand, and dream.

We must always have the desire to learn, grow, and strive for a better version of "me." Somewhere out there are rooms where I must feel small and inadequate in order to be challenged and willing to learn and grow myself. All I have to do is open the door and enter in. There is someone willing to expand me, to teach me, and to help me develop into my destiny through transition!

The process of transition is often complicated but not impossible if you will commit to staying on course. The first and foremost step on the journey to successful transition is letting go of what used to be. This requires honest soul-searching and willingness to admit that it is indeed time to release your control of it.

Most of us are in a time of transition of some form or another. Whether it is by choice or due to circumstances completely out of our control, we are on the path and in the process. The good news is that even if unfortunate occurrences brought you to a transitional stage of life, they could carry you to a time of personal growth, leading to your destiny.

Do you have talents or gifts that you have put on the back burner, hoping to use them "someday," that you could bring back to the forefront now? Were you in a situation that made you feel unimportant or unappreciated? This time could actually lead you to the place in life that will make you realize your value and regain a sense of self-worth.

Nothing stays the same forever. What once was new becomes worn. What was young becomes old, and what was vibrant becomes dull. This is why transition is essential. Anything that is not growing is dying. We must be willing to do things as they have never been done before. Although the gospel never changes, the method by which we present it must change in order to win this new generation to Christ. Let me encourage every reader that transition does not have to be resisted. As a former pastor and current life coach, my greatest joy is helping people become unstuck and move forward into their destinies. Although we never want to forget our heritage, we must also never allow it to dictate our future.

Nothing stays the same forever. What once was new becomes worn. What was young becomes old, and what was vibrant becomes dull.

In all my years as pastor, one thing that remained constant about me was change. I have always loved to keep things moving and exciting! I always wanted to make sure Living Faith avoided falling into the "ruts" that so many churches fall into when they continue to do everything the same way each and every service. One thing no one could ever accuse me of being would be predictable! Even my wife would tease me, saying she would never sit down at home without checking behind her to make sure the chair was still there because I was constantly rearranging the furniture! There were times that I would undergo building projects at the church, not because of necessity, but simply because I knew if we stayed still for too long, we could easily become "stuck" in the place that destroys so many churches—complacency! In ministry, one of our biggest threats is becoming comfortable with where we are. We should always be growing!

The problem with going higher, reaching for greater, or achieving more is that it more than likely brings with it a lot of conflict. It often requires the loss of relationships. Think about the people you associate with the most. If you were to receive a promotion on your job or even start your own business, would they applaud and cheer you on with encouragement or try to talk you out of such "nonsense"? Assessing your closest circle is difficult, but it is necessary.

Anyone can be average, but it takes someone unique and out-of-the-box to do what no one else has done. Sometimes you just have to take a risk! In my studies, I have discovered that an individual fails seven times for every success that they reach. This means that the more you fail, the more you succeed. The only thing worse than failing is never trying at all. In my opinion, you should shoot for the moon, and if you miss, you will still land among the stars. The cemeteries are full of people who lost hope and settled for less than their dreams. Thomas Edison said that he did not fail ten thousand times when creating the light bulb. He simply found 9,999 ways that it didn't work, but he never gave up! Edison had 1,093 patents for different inventions. Many of them, such as the light bulb, the motion picture camera, and the phonograph, were a success considering where we are today. However, the majority of his patents were failures, but because of his determination, today, all of our lives are different! He chose not to just be average as we may know it.

Keep in mind that the road of transition is not a smooth one. It is rough and bumpy, filled with unplanned detours. Most of all, it can be lonely. Others won't understand and may even desert you as you embark on the journey to reach greater heights. But don't let anyone or anything hold you back from your purpose. Transition is far from easy, but it is so rewarding!

At the beginning of my pastoral career, I was constantly with my people. Starting off with just fourteen members, they were my circle of friends. I considered them as family. I attended every ball game and family reunion, helped them move into their homes, and repaired the roofs, constantly making hospital visits and trying to be a superhero of sorts to them. However, as the church began to grow, I was stretching myself too thin and had to put an end to the free home-repair services. Attending every game and birthday party was no longer feasible. Of course, this didn't sit well with some people who were accustomed to me constantly being present. Some of my members became disgruntled, *former* members! This bothered me, of course, but I had to realize that in order to go higher and further towards your goal, you can't hang on to things or people that are holding you back if you truly desire to get to your destiny.

I'm not saying you have to lose every relationship you've ever had in order to soar to your destiny, but I must give fair warning that some people simply can't go with you. There's nothing wrong with them. They aren't bad people. They just can't go. It's not for them. It is for you. Once you have worked up the courage to escape from places or people that are keeping you from achieving your dream, don't look back. Keep your focus on what's ahead of you. Never forget the people who helped you get to different levels in life. But don't spend your time reminiscing to the point that you lose out on those who can be a part of taking you to what God has for your future.

For twenty-seven years, I woke up as the senior pastor and founder of my local congregation. I would roll out of bed with a full schedule every morning and new challenges to face in my growing church in

Forest Park, Georgia. I loved my job, loved my life, and I even loved the challenges that came each day. It was such a blessing to see the congregation grow from a handful of followers to going through seven different building projects that ended with multiple services each Sunday in a sanctuary that seated over 1,100 congregants! For anyone who knew this small-town boy from South Charleston, Ohio, this was a huge success. But, deep down in my soul, I knew my time was coming to an end as the pastor of this thriving ministry. But why change now, especially when things were going so well?

Oftentimes, we are taught to ride the horse until it won't go any farther. But let me encourage you that you do not have to die behind the pulpit of a dying church or leave a company after it goes belly-up. You do not have to leave tired, burned out, or frustrated. You can leave healthy and also leave the church or corporation healthy. Our callings often change heights, and we must be comfortable with that. I believe in my younger days, it was called FAITH and TRUST. Somehow along the journey, we tend to lose a piece of that very vital product that has been entrusted to us. Without faith, it is still impossible to please God.

We are taught that pastors, especially founding pastors, are given a "life sentence" to our churches. CEOs and entrepreneurs can also get caught up in thinking that they can never move on. It can seem strange to move on to something different when things are going great, but I felt a stirring and a shifting in my spirit. Although I had no idea where it was leading, I knew I had to listen to this voice speaking in my heart. It may have seemed as if things were going smoothly on the outside, but things were rumbling on the inside! I was soon going to learn a very valuable lesson in life. Sometimes your ending is really your new beginning!

Many individuals have been amazed at my exit and transition. It is sad, but true, that many were waiting and holding their breath, sure that

I had missed God and would regret my decision to leave what had been the center of my world for so many years. I believe their doubt came from the fact that although I was sure it was time to release my title of Pastor, I had no idea what I was leaving for or going to when I left.

Here I was in a situation where I knew God was sending me away from everything that was familiar to me. This transition was truly a test of my faith. It is one thing to leave a job with the promise of bigger and better. When you have a great salary, an insurance and benefits package, and a 401K in place to help prepare for your retirement years, letting go may not be a huge task. But I had none of that. All I had at this point was God's voice telling me, "Go." However, when God gives you His peace along with that simple instruction, it is much easier to act on it.

Even with the uncertainty of my future, I was reminded of a sermon I had preached years earlier titled, "When the what is clear, the how will appear." It was time to simply trust God. I had the "what." Now, it was time to trust him with the "how." But let me assure you, I did not sit around waiting for manna to fall from heaven to start preparing for an uncertain future ahead. I found a prominent area of Atlanta to rent a business office in, ordered business cards, and got the word out about my coaching business. I honestly had no idea if I would even have one client to ever walk through the doors of my office. I simply knew I had to launch out and take the first step of faith on the journey to whatever it was that God had in store for me. Once we do all we can do, He simply expects us to trust Him for what we can't do.

I am living proof that transition is far from a curse. It is a precious, beautiful blessing!

On December 31, 2016, I passed the baton to my successor: a young, energetic father of five boys, a man full of vision and faith. Then I walked away, full of hope for a bright, beautiful future to come—not just for Pastor Jeremy Tuck and Living Faith Tabernacle, but also for ME and my journey to the great things to come. I now travel the country, as well as internationally, as a coach, mentor, and pastor to other pastors, as a husband to my wife and "Poppy" to my grandchildren, living my dream and leaving a legacy for generations to come after me. I am living proof that transition is far from a curse. It is a precious, beautiful blessing!

Dr. Christopher Bowen is the executive director of Dream Releaser Coaching, a motivational speaker, and travels and speaks internationally. In addition to operating in leadership ministry, he is also a business owner, entrepreneur, teacher, and author.

LEADING TO FOLLOW

LISA POTTER

I wasn't a natural-born leader, not the "Who's Who" of the youth group. When I arrived on the Bible college campus I attended, I was insecure, homesick, unsure of myself, and scared. But I knew I was doing what God wanted me to do and that I was where He wanted me to be. I did not make choir (funny, because I would end up being a worship pastor) or travel with any ministry groups (this was a big deal). I often felt overlooked, and I was afraid to speak up in class.

Everything changed one day. While I was sitting in my missions class, where I remained strategically hidden for fear of being called on, the professor, David Wyns, shared about a class project that would be completed under the direction of five group leaders he would select.

As he called out those names, I was stunned that he had chosen me as one of the five class leaders. I thought, *No, I am not a leader. I am not the one. I have tried to stay hidden from the group so that I am not chosen. Is he not aware that I cannot do this?*

That evening as I contemplated my situation, I determined the only solution was to meet with the professor the next day and plead with him to let me step aside, so the group could be led by someone more capable. When the meeting took place, I came with a carefully written list of all the reasons why I should not be one of the leaders.

When I finished talking, I said, "Professor Wyns, you have picked the wrong person to lead the group."

He responded, "No, Lisa, I have picked the right person. You just don't know it yet."

Moses, during his burning-bush experience, tried to give many convincing arguments to God as to why others would not follow him. The underlying truth for Moses, and for all of us, is that none of these reasons have substance in light of the One who calls:

> In this amazing dialogue Moses experienced the great paradox of calling: God is saying, in essence, it is all about you (because you are the one I have called) and it's not about you at all (because it was all about me and my work in and through you).[6]

An oxymoron is a combination of words that conflict with each other. It is better defined by *Merriam-Webster* as, "a combination of contradictory or incongruous words (as cruel kindness)."[7] The phrase "leading to follow" sounds like an oxymoronic combination, where leading and following are two completely opposite terms. Jesus frequently made these types of statements when He spoke to the disciples or was found teaching the multitudes. For instance, in Mark 8:35 (NIV), "For whoever wants to save his life will lose it, but whoever loses his life for me and for the gospel will save it." I imagine the disciples, upon hearing these words, shaking their heads in one of those "What did He just say?" moments. They had no idea until much later the weightiness of this statement and what it would mean for each of them individually.

When approaching the question, "What does it mean to lead 'Pentecostal-ly?'" I'm convinced it isn't anything like what we perceive it to be. It's the combination of life principles that seemingly look odd

---

6 Ruth Haley Barton, *Strengthening the Soul of Your Leadership* (Downers Grove, IL: InterVarsity Press, 2008), 81.

7 "Oxymoron Definition & Meaning," *Merriam-Webster*, https://www.merriam-webster.com/dictionary/oxymoron.

to the way of the world, where onlookers sort of tilt their heads and say, "That's not the way it's usually done." It's the Leading-to-Follow principle—an upside-down gospel like the one Jesus often spoke about. The answer to the question is in the phrases that don't always make the most sense but are proven over and over in our lives. When these God-breathed principles are pursued, we find them to be kingdom practices that work.

When pondering the phrase "leading Pentecostal-ly," I'm inclined to look at Jesus' leadership principles and the early Acts church that got this Pentecostal movement progressing. How did they operate? What was the DNA of the early church? What principles compelled them to spread the gospel of Christ? What would their vision statement look like? I can't help but think the answers to these questions would look something like this:

VISION STATEMENT: LEADING TO FOLLOW

A) Leading to follow Christ: Let's take up our cross and follow the Jesus model.

B) Leading to follow the Spirit: We don't have much, but we have the Holy Spirit, and that's what we'll give them.

C) Leading to follow the Mission: Let's tell this story to all the world and make more disciples to tell the story.

LEADING TO FOLLOW CHRIST
Our Life: Dying to Self

The word "leading" has a variety of meanings: main, chief, prime, most significant, and most important. When compared to Jesus' leadership model, however, none of these words or phrases seem relevant.

Jesus chose to wash feet before having His feet tended to. He taught a principle of the last being first and the first being last.

Can you imagine what a vision team meeting would look like with the early church team? Peter would have spoken up and said, "Hey, everyone, we are entrusted with this treasure—Jesus left the message with us. What should we do?"

Calling requires us to lead in following Christ, and part of that requirement means dying to self—taking up our cross to follow Jesus. Dying happens early in the calling process, and it happens continuously. I am a little like Peter when it comes to talk of dying: "All this talk of dying, Lord—No!" But Jesus rebuked him and said, "Get thee behind me Satan." Death and dying will always remain part of the process.

> ## Calling requires us to lead in following Christ, and part of that requirement means dying to self—taking up our cross to follow Jesus.

Words such as selfless, sacrificing, giving, and dying are not often used—at least, not by me. The connotations of the words usually bring fear that someday God may hold me accountable for the weightiness of each word. This "dying to self" gospel and the "less of me and more of you" paradigm remains difficult to accept. Who wants to embrace hardship?

Embracing hardship and unwanted circumstances, however, is part of the process of dying to self. It can mean sickness, loss of a loved one, loss of finances, unwillingness to forgive, transition, and so on. The reality remains that we need jostling out of our comfortable place to die to self and lead well.

In calling and leadership, you will experience many "dark nights of the soul," a poignant phrase written by the sixteenth-century priest and poet, St. John of the Cross. Jesus spoke to His disciples about the hard road they would travel. In referring to this, author David Platt writes:

> *On another occasion, right after Jesus commended Peter for his confession of faith in him as "the Christ, the Son of the living God," Jesus rebuked Peter for missing the magnitude of what this means. Like many people today, Peter wanted a Christ without a cross and a Savior without any suffering. So Jesus looked at Peter and the other disciples and said, "If anyone would come after me, he must deny himself and take up his cross and follow me. For whoever wants to save his life will lose it, but whoever loses his life for me will find it."*[8]

The Leading-to-Follow call means having the willingness to go to the hard places, do the hard things, and allow discomfort in life for the sake of the gospel—taking up one's cross and following Him, wherever this may lead and whatever the cost. For the original disciples, it cost them their lives.

In July 2014, my family faced the reality of death with kingdom purpose when my brother died on a mission trip to India. The accident occurred while he, along with men from his church and the missionary, trekked through the Himalayas to share the gospel.

After his death, the missionary recounted a story about Terry that had happened a few days earlier. They met at base camp to review a list of helpful rules to follow for relating to the people and understanding their culture. At the end of the session, Terry approached the missionary privately and said, "At the end of this trip, I'm going to give you another

---

8 David Platt, *Follow Me: A Call to Die. A Call to Live* (Carol Stream, IL: Tyndale House Publishers, Inc., 2013), 11.

one to add to your list." The missionary shared with us later that while he and two other men carried his body on a makeshift stretcher to a nearby village, the thought occurred to him that Terry had written rule number eleven: "It may cost your life, but are you willing to go?"

The Leading-to-Follow call means having the willingness to go to the hard places, do the hard things, and allow discomfort in life for the sake of the gospel.

The idea that you or I will experience literal death for the cause of Christ is unlikely, but Jesus speaks of a spiritual principle that leaders cannot ignore—dying to self. Leaders must take up their cross and follow Jesus. They must lead to follow. While this usually does not make sense, it remains a practice that leaders must apply.

The reciprocal part of calling happens in death. John 12:24 (NIV) states that "unless a kernel of wheat falls to the ground and dies, it remains only a single seed. But if it dies, it produces many seeds." Do seeds dying in order to multiply make any sense? No. But it's a kingdom principle that works. Jesus dying so that we might have life and have it more abundantly is the greatest example that Christ ever gave to us. His life was the ultimate sacrifice for those who will follow Him.

LEADING TO FOLLOW THE SPIRIT
Our Distinctive: The Holy Spirit

Where the previous point often takes us through the fire of refining, this aspect of leading to follow the Spirit pertains more to listening and obeying. It becomes a harder task if we are used to leaning on our natural-born abilities to lead. Let's face the facts: the cream rises to the top, and most of us found in places of leadership within the church structure were leading naturally before we ever stepped into the church. When asked to lead by following the Spirit, we often decline and feel most comfortable relying on our past trial and error.

So, what's the difference between good leadership and Pentecostal leadership? Leadership gives direction and points to the vision. I've been leading since I can remember, leading anyone who would follow. It comes naturally to see a task, organize people, and get everyone running in the same direction to bring about the desired results. Am I good a leader? I hope so. But what makes me a better leader? When I lead to follow the Spirit. When I allow Him to guide my direction and my thoughts. When I rely on the Holy Spirit to say, *This is the way*, and I take up my cross and, in obedience, follow. So, although good leadership can give good direction and vision, leading "Pentecostal-ly" gives God's direction and God's vision.

I'm reminded of a long car ride at the end of a family vacation. We were headed home, the children were sleeping, and my husband and I were discussing the church and confirming our feeling that we were simply spinning our wheels and not actually going anywhere. There was no traction, no direction, and no vision. We desperately needed a right now word from the Holy Spirit. You see, our ability to lead had taken the church and us as far as we could go. If anything was going to propel us into the future, we needed the Holy Spirit to take us there, and more importantly, show us the way.

The longer we drove, the more we prayed, and the Holy Spirit began to fill the space in our car and give us direction. I grabbed a notebook and began to write as my husband spouted off the words. This vision statement, given by the Holy Spirit—in the car—propelled our church into a new realm. We began to see new growth as we saturated our community with "influence... through any means." During this season, this was a huge lesson for both of us. We can lead, but the Holy Spirit leading us is a much better team.

How did the early church accomplish this task? By being continually filled again and again. Being filled with the Spirit over and over. Walking in the Spirit was their life, their conviction, and their purpose. One of my favorite passages is found in Acts 3, where Peter and John are on their way to the temple to pray. They pass by a crippled man, who was daily carried to the temple gate to beg. May I interject here that Jesus would have passed by this gate, this man, many times during his journey through Jerusalem, but He didn't heal him. He could have, but He didn't. But Peter and John arrive on the scene for their time to practice being led by the Spirit. As the crippled beggar cried out for alms, Peter and John looked at him, called his attention to them, and Peter said, "Silver or gold, I do not have, but what I have I give to you. In the name of Jesus Christ of Nazareth, walk" (Acts 3:6, NIV). This was his time, his day to be healed, but more importantly, Peter and John were full of the Holy Spirit, listening to the Holy Spirit, and obedient to the Holy Spirit.

Leading to follow the Spirit is leading being saturated with God's direction and vision.

Jack Hayford stated, "When we talk about the Holy Spirit as rain... the purpose isn't to think, 'Oh the Holy Spirit is like rain.' The purpose is to get wet."[9] Leading to follow the Spirit is leading being saturated with God's direction and vision.

LEADING TO FOLLOW THE MISSION
Our Assignment: Reproduce

The upside-down principle of leading to follow ultimately has to point us to the mission of reproduction. This is not the reproduction of church buildings but the duplication of followers of Christ.

The bare-bones necessity of leading is always follow-ship: the bottom-line standard of leadership that will not change. Jesus started building a team of followers in Mark 1:17 (NIV) with Andrew, "'Come, follow me,' Jesus said, 'and I will send you out to fish for people.'" Andrew followed his leader and brought with him others willing to follow. These harsh and rugged fishermen left their nets to become imitators of Christ.

Leading, as a Pentecostal, must raise the questions, "Who is imitating me?" and "Am I worth imitating?" When our children were little, I was surprised when I would see a gesture or simple quirk that was reminiscent of something my husband or I would do. Since we were their chief influencers, they were duplicating what they saw in us. In the life of the leader, these two questions must be part of the evaluation process. Hebrews 13:7 (AMP) says:

> Remember your leaders [for it was they] who brought you the word of God; and consider the result of their conduct [the outcome of their godly lives], and imitate their faith [their conviction that God exists and is the Creator and Ruler of all things, the Provider of eternal salvation through Christ, and imitate their reliance on God with absolute trust and confidence in His power, wisdom, and goodness].

9 Jack Hayford, "Symbols of the Holy Spirit," *Jack Hayford Ministries*, 19 Nov. 2012, https://www.jackhayford.org/teaching/articles/symbols-of-the-holy-spirit/.

This scripture adds a great responsibility to our mission: people are not just following us, but they are also imitating us. I am aware I'm not capable of this type of scrutiny without the infilling of the Holy Spirit continually in my life. John 3:30 (AMP) must be my prayer: "He must increase [in prominence], but I must decrease." Jesus must grow more prominent; I must grow less so.

This leads us to another key point: our mission is about unity—not separation. My husband has a saying that when the tide comes in, all the boats float. Leading to follow the mission of reproducing followers saturates the church, but more importantly, it overflows into our communities and cities. This overflow of the Spirit's operation in our lives can and should change the spiritual tide over a specific location.

Fortunately, my husband and I were able to spend twenty years as pastors of the same church and community. I make this distinction between church and community because when we resigned the church, the town council and county board of supervisors asked if we would attend their joint session before relocating and leaving this wonderful home of our hearts. We were humbled and honored as the various board and council members thanked us for not just being influencers in our church but for also being influencers in our community. When the tide comes in, all the boats will float. Although accolades are nice when received, ultimately, in the end, it doesn't really matter who gets the credit.

Leading to follow the mission calls us to live in a way that attracts others to follow the Jesus inside of us.

Leading to follow the mission calls us to live in a way that attracts others to follow the Jesus inside of us. It's that burning-bush intersection where we realize that if God is asking us to lead on our own, this could be a disaster. However, if He is coming with us on our mission, the possibilities are endless.

CONCLUSION

Picture with me two large circles, one in each hand. One circle represents "Leadership," and the other circle represents "Pentecostalism." The two are clearly separate entities. To operate effectively, each is not in need of the other; however, taking the two circles, intersecting or interlocking them, they become stronger at the point of intersection. Jesus reminds us in John 15:5b (NIV), "If you remain in me and I in you, you will bear much fruit; apart from me you can do nothing."

As Pentecostal leaders, this intersection between our calling and the Spirit's work in and through us is paramount. It's our burning-bush moment. It is the realization of two important points. First, this calling is about me because HE has called me. Second, it's not about me because HE has called me. It's the puzzling, mystifying reality that causes onlookers to say, "What does that mean?" Yet, for those of us who are living inside the intersection, it's perplexing and sensible at the same time.

We understand it because it is our David-and-Goliath victory balanced by the fact that sometimes we're hiding in a cave for fear of death. It is our crossing-the-Red-Sea triumph but getting to the other side and striking the rock in anger. And it is our Elijah-calling-fire-down-from-heaven success yet ending up defeated by the brook while the ravens feed us.

Do we make it happen? Do we let it happen? I'm not sure of the answer. It is I, but it is more God in me than I alone. Ruth Haley Barton, in *Strengthening the Soul of Your Leadership,* sheds some appropriate insight here:

> *The answer to all of Moses' concerns about why anyone would follow him was simple: The people will follow you because you have met me. Because you know my name deep in your being. That is what qualifies you to be a spiritual leader, and that is why people will be willing to follow you right out of the place they have known for so long to a place that is brand-new.*[10]

Mrs. Lisa Potter is an ordained minister with the Assemblies of God. She is the executive director for Women Who Lead and a graduate of Northpoint Bible College and the Assemblies of God Theological Seminary with an MA in leadership and ministry.

---

10   Ruth Haley Barton, *Strengthening the Soul of Your Leadership* (Downers Grove, IL: InterVarsity Press, 2008) 81.

KILLING MOSES: WHY OLD LEADERSHIP MODELS HAVE TO DIE

MARTIJN van TILBORGH

Most leaders are not opposed to change. In fact, the desire for change is what makes a leader a leader. However, the margin to absorb change is what keeps leaders from actually changing. In other words, the busyness of the day creates a lack of mental capacity to embrace new opportunities that are often hiding in plain sight.

Instead, we tend to spend our time reacting to circumstances in order to keep our organizations stable in the midst of a changing context. This "default" setting has the ability to leave us emotionally, mentally, and even physically bankrupt, resulting in an inability to recognize the need and the opportunity that change can bring.

Change comes at a price—often a high price. And when circumstances seem to stabilize, our fatigued minds tend to rush back to familiar places in an attempt to "catch our breath." However, it's often in these moments that the benefits of change present themselves to us in unexpected ways.

I've come to believe that God Himself puts us in situations where the status quo—our "safe place"—is disrupted in order for us to see opportunities beyond our current reality. The Bible is loaded with stories of leaders who rose to the occasion in the midst of changing circumstances.

God Himself puts us in situations where the status quo—our "safe place"—is disrupted.

A HIGHER ECHELON OF LEADERSHIP

After disruption or crisis, our environment tends to normalize, and there is a tendency to go back to business as usual simply because that seems to be the path of least resistance. Instead, I want to encourage you to leverage this moment to ascend to a new echelon of leadership. Now is the time to rise up and move forward into new opportunities that bring us higher as leaders. If we want to benefit from this moment, we'll have to create enough mental margin in our lives to be able to see the opportunities that are right in front of us.

These new opportunities require the type of change that may forever impact the way we lead. We may be asked to let certain leadership models die in order to fully reap the reward of what's ahead. Moving forward, we simply can't continue to lead the same way—the way that got us to where we are today.

In order to experience new life, something has to die first. It's a universal principle in Scripture that we must understand in order to lead on that next level.

THE DEATH OF AN ERA

What I've described above is not a new concept. It's something that has repeated itself throughout history. God always pushes creation to advance. His kingdom is ever-increasing. As a result, there is a frequent demand for change. The death of something that has served its purpose creates the pathway to new life.

The story of Moses provides us with a prophetic picture of what we're going through today. We can extract many principles and ideas from the life (and death) of Moses that provides us leaders with perspective and clarity.

So, here we go!

MOSES MY SERVANT IS DEAD

Throughout history, Joshua has inspired many leaders with his courage and accomplishments. As a leader, he had the ability to navigate and lead God's people into a place of promise and abundance.

I believe that the key to his great achievements is found in something that God declared to him at the onset of his leadership journey in Joshua 1:2: "Moses my servant is dead. Now then, you and all these people, get ready to cross the Jordan River...."

In order for Joshua to break through into the opportunities available to him across the Jordan, he had to understand the meaning of something that he was already aware of: Moses was dead. Of course, Joshua knew that Moses was dead. Yet God chose to state the obvious in His first instruction to Joshua as he prepared to move into new territory.

Why would God choose to declare something so obvious at the genesis of Joshua's career?

Could it be that Moses had become the epitome of leadership throughout his forty-plus-year career—a career in which he demonstrated success after success to those who followed him? Let's not forget that it was Moses who showed up in Egypt and confronted Pharaoh with signs and wonders, demanding he let God's people go. It was Moses who ascended the mountain and met with God, so he could return with fresh revelation to be shared with the people. And, it was Moses who was able to lead God's people successfully for forty years in unfavorable circumstances.

Many of us would kill for a resume like that of Moses. He was a model leader everyone looked up to. Yet, Moses had to die in order for God's people to reach that next echelon—not just physically but also mentally. After spending forty years under Moses' leadership, Joshua had to accept both Moses' physical death as well as the death of the model of leadership Moses represented. It had fulfilled its purpose. "Moses" had become obsolete for the season they were in. The Moses way of thinking had to be removed from Joshua's mind in order for him to receive the promises God had for him.

Joshua had to accept both Moses' physical death as well as the death of the model of leadership Moses represented.

This new season required a whole new way of thinking and leading. Moses could no longer be used as a point of reference for what successful leadership looked like.

If we allow ourselves to step back and create some mental margin to hear what God has to say to us as leaders, we may hear those same words Joshua heard.

Moses my servant is dead!

Whether we like it or not, whatever got us to where we are can't get us to where we are going! Sooner or later, we've got to align ourselves with the death of the old, even if the old got us to where we are today.

PRINCIPLES OF TRANSITION

When we dive a little deeper into the Moses/Joshua transition, we'll discover several ideas that will help us unlock the mindset needed in order to embrace the same type of change Joshua had to embrace to be successful.

Moses had to be at peace with his death.

In Deuteronomy 32:49-50 (NIV), God told Moses, "'Go up into the Abarim Range to Mount Nebo in Moab, across from Jericho, and . . . die and be gathered to your people.'" Remember, Moses was still alive and kicking when they arrived at the River Jordan. Moses could have been stubborn and kept the reins of his leadership exactly where they had been for the previous forty years. Yet God asked him to go up Mount Nebo to die—to voluntarily lay down his position and venture into a place of certain death.

It took great effort for Moses to climb Mount Nebo. Nothing about it was easy. He had to choose to die in order to position Joshua for success. Moses had to be okay with dying. So he spent the final moments of his life getting to a place that would ultimately kill him.

The people had to be at peace with the new normal.

It's one thing for us as leaders to embrace the changes needed to get to where we're going. It's another thing for the people we lead to do the same. After Joshua had come to peace with Moses' death, his next priority was to get his people on the same page. As leaders, we have to include the people we lead in the mental shifts we're going through in order to get them to follow us in the new season.

Joshua 1 communicates an account of Joshua doing this very effectively, resulting in total alignment of the people with the new vision and model of leadership:

> *Then they answered Joshua, "Whatever you have commanded*
> *us we will do, and wherever you send us we will go. Just as*
> *we fully obeyed Moses, so we will obey you. Only may the*
> *Lord your God be with you as he was with Moses."*
> —Joshua 1:16-17 (NIV)

There was a reason God buried Moses.

Did you know that God Himself buried Moses? You can read about it in Deuteronomy 34:5-6 (NIV):

> *And Moses the servant of the Lord died there in Moab, as the*
> *Lord had said. He buried him in Moab, in the valley opposite*
> *Beth Peor, but to this day no one knows where his grave is.*

In fact, still, nobody knows where his grave is.

Why is this so important? Well, could it be that if Israel had known where Moses' dead body was, they would have applied their faith in an effort to resurrect what God had destined to die? I believe they would have. For more than forty years, Moses had protected them from the dangers of the wilderness—so much so that Moses had become their safe place.

By burying Moses in an unknown place, God would keep Israel (and us) from trying to resurrect the old and push us into applying that faith to new things He has in store for us. This would explain why the devil was contending with the archangel Michael regarding the body of Moses, as we see in the book of Jude verse 9 (NIV): "But even the archangel Michael . . . was disputing with the devil about the body of Moses. . . ."

The devil would love to present us with the body of Moses, so we can be distracted by what will no longer serve us in the future.

CONCLUSION

As church leaders, we have arrived at a place where we can no longer deny the obvious. Moses, God's servant, has died. Not only that, even if we try to find his dead body in hopes of trying to resurrect him, we will be unable to find him. The sooner we allow ourselves to come into alignment with the fact that we've come to the end of an era, the faster we'll reap the benefits of what lies ahead.

> **The sooner we allow ourselves to come into alignment with the fact that we've come to the end of an era, the faster we'll reap the benefits of what lies ahead.**

So let's "kill Moses" by encouraging him to climb that mountain. Let's create margin in our lives to fully embrace the level of change needed in order to move into that next level of command and authority, so we can fully experience what God has in store for us.

Martijn van Tilborgh is a strategic marketing architect and consultant for countless large organizations and well-known individuals. He has also launched many of his own products successfully. An author and speaker, Martijn is always looking to create the NEXT BIG THING in the different niches he works.

7 ATTITUDES OF A SERVANT

PASTOR MARCUS MECUM

"Everybody can be great ... because anybody can serve. You don't have to have a college degree to serve. You don't have to make your subject and verb agree to serve. You only need a heart full of grace. A soul generated by love."
—Martin Luther King, Jr.

Greatness comes in the form of serving. Notice Dr. King didn't use the word "volunteer." There is a significant distinction between "serve" and "volunteer." Greatness comes through *serving*—not *volunteering*.

Jesus said the Son of Man came to *serve* and give His life as a ransom for many (Matthew 20:28). He didn't come to volunteer. In fact, the word volunteer is nowhere to be found in the New Testament. On the other hand, there are hundreds of scriptures on serving.

So, what is the difference between a servant and a volunteer? Attitude.

What is the difference between a servant and a volunteer? Attitude.

There are seven attitudes in particular.

#1—Volunteering is something you *do*. Serving is something you *heart*.

A volunteer tends to focus on the *external*, not the *internal*. Their work is observable from the outside. Servanthood is an invisible attitude because it's on the inside. Volunteers often love recognition for the sacrifices they've made, but a servant isn't worried about recognition. A servant is more concerned with the One who judges the thoughts and intents of the heart (Hebrews 4:12).

Paul says in Colossians 3:23-24 (NIV, emphasis added):

Whatever you do, work at it with all your heart, *as working for the Lord, not for a human master, since you know that you will receive an inheritance from the Lord as a reward.* It is the Lord Christ you are serving.

The heart behind serving is just as important as the act of serving. God is less concerned with the work of your hands in comparison to the work of your heart. At the end of the day, we are serving and working for Him! And we do it with all our heart.

Father, I ask You to give me Your heart. Remind me today that I work for You. Remove my need for validation and recognition from people, and help me to fix my eyes on You!

#2—Volunteers focus on what *they* give. Servants focus on what *Jesus* gave.

Volunteers track the time and energy they spend. And, anything they give cannot be repaid. This means that the organization with which they're volunteering is always in debt to them. A servant doesn't keep track of what they give because Jesus gave it all. Though a volunteer focuses on what they give and the sacrifices they make, a servant is generous because they recognize how generous heaven was toward them, as described in John 3:16 (NIV): "For God so loved the world that he gave his one and only Son. . . ."

Out of the overflow of God's love for the world, He gave the greatest gift anyone could ever ask for. He gifted us Jesus and, thereby, eternal life. A servant is motivated by heaven's generosity and ultimately what Jesus gave on that old rugged cross.

Jesus, thank You for Your sacrifice. Because of what You gave, I GET to give. I'm so grateful for your generosity in my life. Help me to focus on Your sacrifice and the price You paid.

#3—Volunteers keep *score*. Servants make *sacrifices*.

Volunteers love to keep score. Isaiah 14 tells us that Lucifer said in his heart:

"I will ascend to heaven;
above the stars of God.
I will set my throne on high;
I will sit on the mount of assembly
in the far reaches of the north;
I will ascend above the heights of the clouds;
I will make myself like the Most High."
—Isaiah 14:13-14 (ESV)

"I, I, I." An "I" mentality will bring division to anything God wants to do. A servant's attitude makes sacrifices and keeps no record of wrongs (1 Corinthians 13:5). Servants deny themselves, take up their cross, and follow Jesus (Matthew 16:24). They don't keep score. They don't need the tasks that are most desirable, recognizable, or glorious. They're here to sacrifice and serve. They recognize that the unseen parts of the body are the most vital (1 Corinthians 12:22).

Lord, remove any selfish desires in my heart. Help me to NOT keep score. Take away any "I" mentality that may exist in me. I want You to receive all the glory and honor that You deserve.

#4—Volunteers are *time-sensitive*. Servants are *need-sensitive*.

Volunteers are overly sensitive to time. They focus on how much time they spend volunteering. They focus on volunteering at times that are most convenient for them. For a volunteer, everything comes down to time. A servant, on the other hand, is "need" sensitive. They care more about the needs of the organization they're serving than the time spent serving. A servant finds and meets the need regardless of time.

Jesus talked about this very principle in the parable of the Good Samaritan (Luke 10:25-37). There was a man who'd been beaten, robbed, and left for dead. Religious people saw the need but passed by the man. I'm sure they had an excuse, and I'm sure it was a good excuse.

Bottom line, it was inconvenient for them. They assumed someone else would do it. Someone else would help the man and meet the need. Then, the Good Samaritan walked by and met the need. He used whatever resources he had available to help the hurting man.

Jesus calls us to have mercy, show empathy, and meet the needs of the people we serve.

When looking at the actions and the heart of the Good Samaritan, Jesus calls us to *go and do likewise* (Luke 10:37). He calls us to have mercy, show empathy, and meet the needs of the people we serve.

Father, help me to be sensitive to the needs of Your people. I don't want to pass by a hurting person because of my busyness. I don't want to lose focus on the importance of reaching people.

#5—A volunteer wants to look good. A servant wants *God* to look good.

Serving isn't about the servant receiving glory. Serving is about God receiving glory through what we do. Matthew 5:14-16 reminds us of this principle:

"You are the light of the world. A town built on a hill cannot be hidden. Neither do people light a lamp and put it under a bowl. Instead they put it on its stand, and it gives light to everyone in the house. In the same way, let your light shine before others, that they may see your good deeds and glorify your Father in heaven."
—Matthew 5:14-16 (NIV, emphasis added)

The world should see our good deeds and glorify God! Our job is to make Jesus famous—to bring Him the honor and glory He deserves. A servant wants to make God look good. Our light isn't for others to see us. A servant isn't interested in shedding light on their work and efforts. Our light helps others see Him! We're trying to shed light on the goodness and mercy of our God!

Father, let my light shine before others so that they see Your goodness and Your mercy. I'm not interested in shedding light on my own efforts and work. I want You to receive all the glory and honor. Lord, let my actions lead people to You.

#6—Volunteering is about *convenience*. Serving is about *commitment*.

There is a story in 2 Kings about a group of people that traveled a particular path, but every time they traveled the path, they were attacked by lions. So, they went to the Lord in prayer and asked Him to protect them from the lions. God responded with protection. Later in this chapter, the Bible says something very interesting: "Even while these people were worshiping the Lord, they were serving their idols" (2 Kings 17:41, NIV).

This group of people wanted just enough God to keep the lions away. Just enough God to meet their needs. They wanted God on their terms. And if we're not careful, that is what happens to us. We want God's protection. We want His favor. But Monday through Friday, we serve our own gods. We want to be *connected* to God without being *committed* to God.

Where a volunteer is *connected* and *involved*, a servant is *committed*.

Lord, I am here to serve You. Help me remove any idols in my life so that my commitment is to You alone. I will serve You no matter the cost or the convenience because You are worthy.

#7—Volunteering makes you *superior*. Serving makes you *humble*.

Volunteers love position. Especially position that makes them superior. However, serving is never big "I"s and little "you"s. The church isn't made up of one-man superstars. Romans 12:4-5 (NIV) says:

> *For just as each of us has one body with many members, and these members do not all have the same function, so in Christ we, though many, form one body, and each member belongs to all the others.*

The church is a body with many members. Each member plays their unique part. Paul went on to say in 1 Corinthians 12:21 (NIV) that "the eye can't say to the hand, 'I don't need you!' And the head can't say to the feet, 'I don't need you!'" We need each other!

There is no superiority in serving. In fact, it's the opposite. Serving makes you humble. When you serve someone, you humble yourself. When pride walks in a church, God walks out. Paul put it this way: "Do nothing out of selfish ambition or vain conceit. Rather, in humility value others above yourselves" (Philippians 2:3, NIV).

Do nothing out of selfish ambition. A servant is mindful of others. The New American Standard Bible says, "With humility consider one another *as more important than yourselves*" (emphasis added). Imagine a world where people consider others as more important than them-selves. Servants treat each person they encounter as if they're the most important person in the room.

Lord, humble me. Help me to prioritize the needs of others. Show me how to consider others more important than myself, and teach me to look to the interests of others above my own.

Jesus is our model and motivation for serving.

Jesus is our model and motivation for serving. Everywhere He went, people were on His mind. When He met some of His first disciples in Matthew 4, Jesus told them, "Hey, you've had fish on your mind. But, if you follow Me, you'll have people on your mind for the rest of your life. I'll change your mind and the way you think about people. Going forward, you'll be fishers of people" (author paraphrase).

Jesus had people on His mind. He *wasn't* thinking about His title or His position. He thought about people.

When Lazarus died and Jesus saw Mary weeping over the death of her brother, the Bible says in John 11:35 (NIV), "Jesus wept." And the Jews watching this unfold were amazed at Jesus' love for people. People were on His mind.

Even on the cross, Jesus had people on His mind. He had His mother's welfare on His mind. He told John to take care of His mom while He was gone. He had the thief beside Him on His mind. He told one of the thieves they would be with Him in paradise. He even had the people who nailed Him to the cross on His mind. He said the famous prayer, "Father, forgive [these *people*] for they don't know what they're doing" (Luke 23:34, NLT, emphasis added).

Jesus always had people on His mind, and *we have the mind of Christ* (1 Corinthians 2:16). Our leadership is only as good as our love for people. Jesus put it this way: "Everyone will know that you are my disciples, *by your love for people*" (John 13:35, author paraphrase).

Lord, we want to love people like You loved people. We recognize the true mark of a follower of Christ is their love for people. Help us to love people like we've never loved people before. We want the attitude of a servant. We thank You for the example You set for us—ultimately laying your life down for Your creation. May our lives be a living sacrifice for You. May our serving bring YOU glory, and may our attitudes be those of a servant, in Jesus' name!

Pastor Marcus Mecum is the founder and senior pastor of 7 Hills Church. He has led 7 Hills in following Christ and loving their community for over 15 years. Pastor Marcus's prayer is to see the body of Christ truly living out its call to be the hands and feet of Jesus to one another and the world around them.

LIGHT A FIRE

PASTOR JIM CYMBALA

UNCONDITIONAL SURRENDER

"I consider my life worth nothing to me; my only aim is to finish the race and complete the task the Lord Jesus has given to me—the task of testifying to the good news of God's grace."
—Acts 20:24 (NIV)

When the Japanese bombed Pearl Harbor on December 7, 1941—the date that Franklin D. Roosevelt said would "live in infamy"—the United States suddenly found itself plunged into a situation it had tried very hard to avoid. Things looked grim for the US at that point: the better part of its naval force had been destroyed, and the Germans had honored their treaty with Japan and declared war against the US, effectively forcing the country into two major wars on opposite sides of the globe.

By 1944, the Japanese realized that they had picked a fight with the wrong enemy. Their military resources dwindled, as did their force numbers. They grew increasingly desperate. In October of that year, they stunned the world and nearly changed the tide of the war when they unveiled a frightening new weapon. Unable to compete with US airpower—in terms of both quality and quantity—the Japanese nevertheless started producing flimsy planes as fast as they could. These planes held two deadly secrets. The first was a bomb placed inside the nose of the plane. The second was a pilot who had sworn a sacred oath to the Emperor to fly the plane directly into battleships and aircraft carriers. In effect, Japan deployed a massive force of pilot-guided explosives. So many Japanese men were willing to face certain death in dedication to their Emperor, whom they held as divine, that the Imperial Japanese Army couldn't build the planes fast enough. The program—which became known under the name *kamikaze* ("divine wind")—had a devastating impact. Before Japan finally ran out of the materials necessary to build the planes, *kamikazes* had flown some 3,800 suicide missions and taken the lives of more than seven thousand Allied sailors and other naval personnel.

The *kamikaze* program illustrates an important fact. When you find yourself face-to-face with an opponent who truly doesn't care if they live or die so long as they complete their mission, you've got a real problem on your hands. You can't threaten or intimidate them. You can't buy them off or negotiate with them. And when a believer becomes someone who doesn't care if they live or die, they become a powerful weapon in the hand of God.

When a believer becomes someone who doesn't care if they live or die, they become a powerful weapon in the hand of God.

Paul addressed the Ephesian elders in Acts 20:24 (NIV), saying, "I consider my life worth nothing to me." Although his friends didn't want to see him chained and thrown into prison, Paul didn't seem to care. He was going to follow Jesus no matter what. I wonder what we would think about Paul today. Would we accept him? Call him a fanatic? Push him to the sidelines and pretend he's not there?

Or would we be inspired and follow his example?

EYES ON ETERNITY

We tell ourselves—we preach to our congregations—that life is just a vapor while heaven with Christ is eternal. Therefore, we shouldn't consider this life as all-important. But few live that way, right? We live as if this earthly life were forever. As if we couldn't afford to lose it. When a Christian dies, we treat it as a horrible tragedy. Yet Psalm 116:15 (NIV) declares, "Precious in the sight of the Lord is the death of his faithful servants."

Our perspective, even as pastors, is often earthbound. We've got our sermons to preach, our programs to administer, our vacations and retirement plans to look forward to. But there's a far different attitude toward ministry described in the New Testament. You can see it in the lives of Paul and the other apostles. They had a radical belief in an invisible God and in the eternal rewards that await us when this life is over.

I once visited Hong Kong, where I had been invited to speak to a couple of hundred pastors of underground churches in mainland China. I was told that half of them had been in prison because of their allegiance to Christ. To be honest, I felt unworthy to address them. I thought, *Who am I to talk to them? I've never faced the prospect of being thrown in prison for preaching the gospel of Christ.*

The worship was simple but glorious. There were just a couple of guitar players in front leading it. Something about the way those pastors were singing touched me deeply. They were looking upward as if they could actually see Jesus.

I loved the melody of one of the choruses they were singing and asked my interpreter what the words were. I don't have the exact translation, but it went something like this: "Lord, thank you for loving us so much that you came and gave your life for us. And because of your love, we love you back. So, we're ready to die. We dedicate our lives to you whether we live or die."

Not exactly the typical praise and worship chorus that we hear on a Sunday morning in America.

I found myself praying: "God, is there any way you could get me out of delivering this message? I really would prefer not to speak. I don't feel worthy to teach these people. And their worship is so beautiful. I would rather just keep worshiping you with them."

Well, God chose not to excuse me from speaking, and I went ahead with my message. I hope it was helpful to them, and I remember those pastors often when I'm facing a challenge. They were among the happiest Christians I'd ever met. And yet, many had to meet in secret. In America, we think it's a major trial when the transmission goes bad in our automobiles. We live pampered lives compared to those brave soldiers. They had to face the prospect of prison. They were singing, "Yes, Lord, I will gladly die for you." For them, that wasn't just a nice sentiment. It was a very real possibility.

Are we familiar with this kind of consecration: "I have only one mission. I want to do the will of God. And if it costs me my life, so be it"? And is that kind of devotion still possible today?

LOVING THE FORSAKEN

I want to tell you about a young woman from our church whom we'll call Mary. She was introduced to me several years ago by our missions pastor. "Pastor," he said, "this young woman feels called to the mission field. The other pastors and I have met with her. We think she's ready, and we'd like you to meet her."

I asked him where she wanted to go and what she felt called to do. He said she wasn't sure. She only knew that she wanted to go to the Middle East and that she had a burden for people who were forsaken and forgotten.

We prayed for Mary and sent her out. She ended up working mostly among the Yazidi people in the internally displaced people camps in the Middle East. The Yazidis have a primitive animistic religion that is despised by the surrounding Muslim population. They are treated with contempt by everyone around them, viewed as the offscouring of humanity.[11]

Mary went to teach English, ostensibly, and to work with the Yazidi women. Life is especially brutal for the Yazidi women. When attacked by ISIS forces, they are treated as spoils of war. Yazidi women who convert to Islam are sold as brides. Those who refuse to convert are tortured, raped, and sometimes murdered.

We got regular reports from Mary. The work was going well. My heart was blessed by her dedication. She had left everything behind and risked everything to serve Jesus and do His will.

Mary came back to New York for a brief sabbatical about three years later. I asked her how it was going. As she summarized her work among the Yazidis, she casually added a note about a growing difficulty.

"As an outsider, many assume I must be involved in the sex trade. They talk nasty to me. Especially the taxi drivers." Taxi drivers? Why was she taking taxis? I then learned that was the only way for her to get around. She didn't own a car.

That night Mary came to our weekly prayer meeting. I brought her up to give an update on her work and then prayed for the offering.

---

11 "Yazidis," *Wikipedia*, Wikimedia Foundation, 27 Apr. 2022, https://en.wikipedia.org/wiki/Yazidis.

She shared very briefly, describing how she worked with women who were looked down on and treated miserably. She related how she loved them and shared Jesus with them along with teaching English. Then she prayed. Before the collection began, I explained that beyond our regular support, a part of that offering would go to her as a special gift. And I shared her problem and need, telling the group about the taxi drivers who had talked inappropriately to her. "Let's believe God for the car she needs," I said. And then we went on with the service.

Providentially, there was a group of pastors from Colorado visiting that night. The instant the meeting ended, they came up to me. "We've just talked together," they said, "and we want to buy Mary the automobile she needs." And they did. Later, we sent those pastors a picture of the car they had made possible, and our entire church rejoiced over God's provision for her.

Looking back, how could we not try to help someone who was serving the Lord, caring little for her own comfort and safety?

CONSECRATED TO GOD

One word for what Paul was discussing in Acts 20:24—considering our lives as worth nothing to ourselves—is *consecration*. To be consecrated means to be dedicated solely and entirely and irrevocably to God. This is what Paul urged the Christians in Rome to be: "Therefore, I urge you, brothers and sisters, in view of God's mercy, to offer your bodies as a living sacrifice, holy and pleasing to God—this is your true and proper worship" (Romans 12:1, NIV).

What God wants most from each one of us is not a financial offering or occasional service in the church. Jesus surrendered Himself and died for us, and now He asks us to surrender *our* lives as a pleasing sacrifice to Him. What could be more reasonable? After He gave His life for us on the cross, is it enough for us to respond by merely devoting some of our time or a portion of our finances? No. The kind of consecration we're talking about here must be something we choose to do—a decision we consciously make. God won't compel us to do it against our will. Returning to the warfare theme from the start of this chapter, we have to know that God will not "draft" us into His army. What made the Japanese *kamikaze* pilots so frightening and so dangerous was that they were not forced into fighting; they *voluntarily* swore themselves to obey the Emperor.

Jesus surrendered Himself and died for us, and now He asks us to surrender our lives as a pleasing sacrifice to Him.

General William Booth, founder of the Salvation Army, once said that "the greatness of a man's power is the measure of his surrender." But surrendering our lives is not something we can accomplish on our own. The self-life never wants to give up its rights in full submission to the Lord. And Jesus regularly commanded us to do things that are impossible for us. For example, Christ said, "As I have loved you, so you must love one another" (John 13:34, NIV). Does He really expect us to love one another with the same exact love He has shown us? Yes! But apart from the power of the Holy Spirit, this is absolutely impossible. Here's the good news, however: Just as *all merit* is in the Son, for He alone gives us acceptance with God, *all power* is by the Spirit, who gives us the willingness and ability to obey all God asks of us. Human effort will not suffice.

Just as you and I cannot possibly love one another as Christ has loved us without the help of the Holy Spirit, we can't grit our teeth and will ourselves to "present [our] bodies as a living sacrifice" (Romans 12:1) in absolute surrender. As E. M. Bounds said, "The power to consecrate can only be communicated by the Holy Ghost." We need to be asking God continually for the grace needed to accomplish this consecration: "Lord, give me a heart totally dedicated to you, no matter what."

BLESSED ARE THE BEGGARS

Think about this for a moment. Before there was any creation, who existed? God. All good that existed was in God. All love that existed was in God. Everything, by definition, had to come from God. Then Adam and Eve were created. What was their first consciousness? Who was ever in a better position to appreciate that all things come from God? "We exist because of him. This breath? He gave it to us. All this vegetation, all these animals? He gave them to us." Who else could ever have understood so clearly that everything around them—including their own lives—was a gift?

God's plan of salvation through Christ was to bring us back to that original consciousness—to see and know that everything comes from Him, and we were created as receiving vessels only. *He* is the giver of every good and perfect gift (James 1:17). The strongest Christians and the most mature believers are merely the ones who have received the most from God. They have learned the secret that everything must come from the Lord as a gift.

The very first thing Jesus taught His followers was "Blessed are the poor in spirit, for theirs is the kingdom of heaven" (Matthew 5:3, NIV). There are two Greek words for "poor" in the New Testament. One indicates someone who has to work hard every day just to buy enough to eat. The other one is used for people who have nothing at all. They can only beg to get through the day. Which word do you think Jesus used in the beatitude? Amazingly, he used the second word. Here's one possible rendering of the beatitude: "Blessed are the beggars, for theirs is the kingdom of heaven"! All that God has is available to them because their poverty of spirit makes them totally dependent on Him.

I wish I had known this when I first went into the ministry. It's not about my trying harder to preach better. It's not about relying on my own strength to better organize my work and schedule. It's all about asking and receiving. Oh, how that reality obliterates our pride! The greatest ministers, the most spiritual believers, are the ones who have received the most because they're constantly seeking God out of their deep sense of need. They can't boast. How can anyone boast in something they had to ask for and receive from God as a gift?

It's all about asking and receiving. Oh, how that reality obliterates our pride!

"IT'S ALWAYS TOO SOON TO QUIT"

Paul continued by saying that his only aim was "to finish the race and complete the task the Lord Jesus has given to me" (Acts 20:24, NIV). It's important to note that he didn't say he wanted to "start" the race or "begin" the task. He didn't say he wanted to "continue" the race or "keep pursuing" the task. He wanted to *finish* the race and *complete* the task.

In almost all ministers' lives, there comes a time when Satan tries to get them to quit before they cross the finish line. When I was only a year or so in the ministry, I got so discouraged I tried to resign from the church. My preaching was bad. We were in a run-down building in a poor neighborhood. The building was nearly empty, and the offerings were pitifully low at every service. I felt like I just couldn't continue. I didn't succeed in resigning my post, but only because the Lord graciously blocked my way. Twice I tried to do something else to support my family, but in both cases, God had the interview appointments canceled at the last moment. I got the message loud and clear: It's always too soon to quit.

It's not just in difficult beginnings that we are challenged. Some pastors secretly give up at the other end of the journey. I know people who've been in ministry for twenty-five years or more. They're still in their churches, still drawing their pay, and still going through the motions. But in fact, deep inside where it counts, they've already retired. One of them said to me, "I just don't want to hear about people's problems anymore." Does he still preach? Yes. Is it doctrinally correct? Yes. Is his heart in it? No. He's not really running the race anymore; he's just running out the clock.

In his letter addressed to Philemon, Paul sent regards to "Apphia our sister and Archippus our fellow soldier" (Philemon 1:2, NIV). We're not told anything more about either of them. Many commentators believe that Apphia was Philemon's wife and that Archippus was their son. We do know, however, that Archippus had a ministry role in the church at Colossae.

In his letter to the Christians there, Paul wrote, "Tell Archippus: 'See to it that you complete the ministry you have received in the Lord'" (Colossians 4:17, NIV). These words were read publicly to the church with the rest of the letter. It may have been a gentle rebuke for having neglected some of his duties or a strong word of encouragement to a fellow soldier who had grown weary or discouraged. Either way, Paul told Archippus to "complete" the ministry the Lord had given him. He had already begun his assignment; now, he needed to complete it.

This is a word that we can share with those who minister alongside us. It certainly is a word that we can receive as addressed personally to each of us, who are also Paul's "fellow soldiers."

TRUE SUCCESS

Paul also said in Acts 20:24 (NIV) that he wanted to "complete the task that the Lord Jesus has given me." This refers to a personal commission that Paul received from the Lord. Scripture tells us there is what we might call a "general" will of God: one that applies to all Christians equally. For instance, Jesus told us to "[l]ove one another" (John 13:34, NIV). That is true for all Christians at all times. Or when Paul said, "For this is the *will* of God, your sanctification; that is, that you abstain from sexual immorality" (1 Thessalonians 4:3, ESV). Or again: "In everything give thanks; for this is God's *will* for you in Christ Jesus" (1 Thessalonians 5:18, NASB, emphasis added). Every believer should accept these commands as God's will for their lives.

But Scripture also makes it clear that God has a personal will for each of us individually involving the unique task that has been given to us and the path we are to closely follow. Whom should we marry? Where should we live? As believers, where should we serve in the body of Christ? Is the offer to pastor another church really from God? Nobody knows God's individual will for each of us but God. And thankfully, the Lord wants us to know His plan for our lives. As we humbly trust Him, He will direct our paths.

In light of this, what is the definition of success? Success in life consists of nothing more than finding the will of God and then doing it. If God's will is that we minister in a small town in the upper Midwest, in a large city, or on a foreign mission field, success for us will mean doing precisely that—regardless of our preferences, other people's expectations, or the world's definition of having "made it."

Some Christians, though not necessarily called to public ministry, could very possibly bring greater joy to God's heart than those in leadership. They have discovered God's plan for their lives and totally given themselves over to it. That means a deacon or choir member might receive a greater reward than the pastor of the church.

I think we can all agree that Jesus lived His entire life in the perfect will of God. But think about this: What was Jesus doing when he was twenty-seven years old? Was He calling disciples to follow Him? Was He healing people? Working miracles? No. He was doing none of those things. But His life was successful because the perfect will of God for Him was to wait in Nazareth until the right time came to begin His public ministry. It is noteworthy that when He was being baptized by John in the Jordan River, before He entered into public ministry, Jesus heard the Father say, "This is my Son, whom I love; with him I am well pleased" (Matthew 3:17, NIV).

Too many ministers have the idea that success is nothing more than the carnal "American dream," —advancement, fame, fortune—and whose model for success is someone wearing $400 sneakers, living extravagantly, and hanging out with celebrities and politicians. What they call great is actually a sign that they've lost their way.

God's will for our lives is between Him and us. Each day we can simply walk with the one who sent us on our mission. Draw near to Him. Listen to the Spirit's voice. There is a trap in desiring approval from people. In the end, the approval we need must come from Jesus.

Are we in the perfect will of God today? Are we seeking to know this personal plan for our lives, a plan that existed even before we were born? Are we trusting the Holy Spirit for the grace to do the will of God as it is revealed to us? The highest form of worshiping God has nothing to do with praise choruses or lying prostrate on the floor. What the Father delights in most is that which was written concerning His own Son:

Therefore, when Christ came into the world, he said:
"Sacrifice and offering you did not desire,
but a body you prepared for me;
with burnt offerings and sin offerings
you were not pleased.
Then I said, 'Here I am—it is written about me in the scroll—
I have come to do your will, my God.'"
—Hebrews 10:5-7 (NIV, emphasis added)

The truth is, sometimes doing the will of God is not so easy. I remember an instance many years ago when I found myself at ten o'clock on a Saturday night with no sermon for Sunday. No matter what I tried, the heavens seemed as brass—not a word. I prayed, "God, please help me. Is there something in me hindering Your Spirit?" Immediately, God brought to mind my relationship with three people who had grown distant from me. It's as if a silent wall had been erected. No big fight or feud, just a sense that something wasn't the way it should be.

I sensed that God was saying, *Call them and ask for forgiveness.*

"What? Call them? Now? Isn't it too late in the evening for that? And you know, in two cases for sure, they're the ones needing to apologize." The fact is, my pride was ruffled at the idea that I was somehow in the wrong.

Do you want My blessing? Then do My will. Make it right.

I took a deep breath and called the first person. I was secretly hoping that he might not pick up. But he did.

"Uh, hi," I said. "It's Jim."

"Hi, how are you?"

"I'm good. Listen, there's something I want to say to you. I have this gnawing feeling that something may be wrong between us. If there's anything I've said or done that hurt you or offended you, I'm sorry. Please forgive me."

To my surprise, he said, "Frankly, I've had the same feeling. There's nothing you've done that you need to apologize for. But if there's anything I've done that has hurt *you*, I apologize as well." We had a brief prayer together, and that was that.

The same thing happened with the other two people.

I felt that a great burden had been lifted. And, yes, I did get direction and help for the next day. Was it hard to make those calls? Absolutely. But God has promised us grace to accomplish His will.

We will never be happier than when we're in the center of God's will.

I have been blessed to have traveled a lot in my life, not only around our country, but also on numerous trips overseas. There are some beautiful places on this earth, but let me tell you about the best place you could ever live—the center of God's will. Will there be satanic attacks? For sure. Challenging days filled with mountains blocking your way? Absolutely. But the joy is inexpressible, and the peace you find there is fathomless. We will never be happier than when we're in the center of God's will.

Pastor Jim Cymbala has served as the senior pastor of the Brooklyn Tabernacle in New York City, NY, since 1971. At the beginning of his tenure, church membership numbered fewer than 30 people and has grown to more than 16,000 members under Pastor Cymbala's leadership.

LEADERSHIP PAIN

SAM CHAND

I t's inevitable, inescapable. By its very nature, leadership produces change, and change—even wonderful growth and progress—always involves at least a measure of confusion, loss, and resistance. To put it another way, leadership that doesn't produce pain is either in a short season of unusual blessing, or it isn't really making a difference. So,

Growth = Change

Change = Loss

Loss = Pain

Thus, Growth = Pain

When leaders in any field take the risk of moving individuals and organizations from one stage to another—from stagnation to effectiveness or from success to significance—they inevitably encounter confusion, passivity, and outright resistance from those they're trying to lead. It's entirely predictable. Any study of business leaders shows this pattern in the responses of team members. Pastors' teams and congregations are no exception. The long history of the church shows that God's people are, if anything, even *more* confused, *more* passive, and *more* resistant when their leaders point the way to fulfill God's purposes. Organizational guru Peter Drucker observed that the four most difficult jobs in America are, in no particular order: president of the United States, university president, hospital CEO, and pastor. (I've been in two of these roles: pastor and university president.) If you're a church leader and struggling in your role, you're in good company!

The normal human response to pain is to do anything except face it.

The normal human response to pain is to do anything except face it. We *minimize* the problem ("Oh, it's not really that bad."), *excuse* those who have hurt us ("She didn't really mean it."), or *deny* it even happened ("What conflict? What betrayal? What hurt? I don't know what you're talking about!").

LEADERSHIP LEPROSY

But pain isn't the enemy. The inability or unwillingness to face pain is a far greater danger. I grew up in India where I saw thousands of lepers. They are often missing noses, ears, fingers, and toes—but not because their flesh rots away. (That's a common misconception.) Various body parts become severely damaged because they don't sense the warning signs of pain to stay away from dangers. Dr. Paul Brand worked with lepers in India and the United States. In *The Gift of Pain*, coauthored with Philip Yancey, Brand tells the story of four-year-old Tanya. When her mother brought Tanya to the national leprosy hospital in Carville, Louisiana, Dr. Brand immediately noticed the little girl appeared totally calm as he removed her bloodstained bandages and examined her dislocated ankle. As the doctor gently moved her foot to assess the extent of the damage, Tanya appeared bored. She felt no pain at all.

Tanya suffered from a rare genetic malady called congenital indifference to pain, a condition very similar to leprosy. In every other way, she was a healthy little girl, but she felt no pain at all. Years earlier, Tanya's father left because he couldn't handle the stress of raising her—he had called her "a monster." Dr. Brand observed, "Tanya was no monster, only an extreme example—a human metaphor, really—of life without pain."[12]

Tanya and millions of others without the capacity to feel pain endure a severe, involuntary handicap, but the rest of us often choose to be numb and suffer the consequences. Many leaders think they have to put on a happy face (or at least a stoic face) for the people in their organizations, so they refuse to admit their discouragement, disappointment, and disillusionment—even to themselves—or they try to delay their pain. They tell their worried (and maybe angry) spouse, "As soon as the building campaign is over, the new music program is in place, the new staff member is hired, or some other benchmark is achieved, I can slow down and the stress will subside." For pastors and all other leaders, ignoring pain is leadership leprosy. It may promise the short-term gain of avoiding discomfort, but it has devastating long-term consequences.

For church leaders, pain is pervasive and persistent. People who are involved in any form of church leadership, and especially pastors, see more of the underbelly of life than members of any other profession. Insurance agents see those who come to them for protection against loss, bankers and mortgage brokers see people who have financial needs, doctors treat physical problems, and mechanics look under the car hood—none of them look into peoples' hearts like a pastor does. None of these people see people at the apogee and perigee of their lives—times of greatest celebrations, like weddings and births, and times of deepest loss, like divorce, disease, and death. Pastors are

---

12 Paul Brand and Philip Yancey, *The Gift of Pain* (Grand Rapids: Zondervan, 1997), 3–5.

exposed to the highest hopes and the deepest wounds of those in their care. And it's not temporary; it's from the womb to the tomb.

Pastors are exposed to the highest hopes and the deepest wounds of those in their care. And it's not temporary; it's from the womb to the tomb.

Making friends with your pain is part of leadership. Our pains tell us we're moving in the right direction. New pains will always be a part of your life as you continue climbing the ladder to your destiny.

Do you want to be a better leader? Raise the threshold of your pain. Do you want your church to grow? Do you want your business to reach higher goals? Reluctance to face pain is your greatest limitation. There is no growth without change, no change without loss, and no loss without pain. You and your organization will grow only to—and not a step beyond—your pain threshold. If you're not hurting, you're not leading. Your vision for the future has to be big enough to propel you to face the heartaches and struggles you'll find along the way.

MY STORY

Sometimes, the culture where we live is backward, stunted, and repressive. Prejudice inflicts enormous pain. In the early '70s, when I was a janitor at Beulah Heights Bible College, one of my duties was to go to every office and pick up the trash. During the first week, when I went to the dean's office, I saw a lovely young lady who was his executive assistant. Oh, she looked nice! I introduced myself. She replied sweetly,

"My name is Brenda." Like any other lovestruck young man, I began to strategize how I could get to know her and take her out. But there was a problem: Brenda is Caucasian, and I'm Indian. Brenda and I met about ten years after President Johnson signed the Civil Rights Act, but it appeared that some people in Georgia had never heard of racial equality!

I didn't have enough money to date Brenda, but the mere fact that I obviously liked her sent ripples of tension throughout the campus. In response, the college's board met in an urgent session and passed a policy to forbid people from dating outside their ethnicity. That, they soon realized, wasn't clear enough. They needed to define "dating." They defined it as having a conversation longer than five minutes, sitting at the same cafeteria table, riding in the same car, sitting next to each other in class, or sitting in the same church pew. In effect, the board members tried to establish an exclusion zone expressly designed to keep me away from Brenda.

Brenda and I respected the leadership of the college, but we also wanted to continue to see each other. On three occasions, the dean, acting on behalf of the college board, called us into his office and threatened to expel us if we continued to talk to each other. Expulsion would be uncomfortable for Brenda but catastrophic for me. She could attend any other school in the country. The move would require some relocation and interruption, but her life wouldn't be upset for very long. On the other hand, if I were expelled, I would lose my student visa and be deported. Under the terms of the government, I would never be allowed to enter the United States again for the rest of my life.

Another dean on campus, who was the designated counselor for the students, occasionally called Brenda to come to see him. He told her that if she kept seeing me, she would go to hell. (I'm not kidding or exaggerating.) Brenda has great respect for authority, so she left these meetings crushed with guilt and confusion. After each one, she told me she had to break up with me because she didn't want to go to hell. After a while, she realized the dean was using these threats to manipulate her, and we got back together. This happened several times.

Brenda and I have boxes full of notes we wrote each other during our time at Beulah Heights Bible College. When we couldn't see each other, we wrote or called. The phones in our two dorms were only about twenty yards apart, but using them was safer than meeting face-to-face. Our dance of love and secrecy lasted for three years. We both took risks, but they were worth it.

One year on Secretaries Appreciation Day, I was sure no one would acknowledge Brenda and thank her for her faithful and excellent service, so I used the little money I'd saved to buy a bouquet of flowers and have them delivered to her desk. Someone noticed the pretty flowers and asked her, "Who gave these to you? They're beautiful!"

Without thinking, she answered, "Sam did!" When word spread, we both got a summons from the dean.

I was brought up in a culture that deeply respects those who are in authority. India is a gracious land that gives the highest honor to parents, teachers, and other leaders. In every threatening conversation with the dean, I never barked back or stormed out. I sat quietly and listened, and when he was finished, I said, "Thank you, sir." Even as a young man in college, I understood that the fear and racism evident on the board didn't appear out of a vacuum. To a great degree, those men were the products of their culture. They had lived with Jim Crow laws; I hadn't. They had seen marches and police brutality; I hadn't. They had watched as Martin Luther King, Jr., and Bobby Kennedy were buried; I had come to an America that had suffered enormous pain and fear.

During those awful years when I was a student, I believed the leadership and the board of the school were ignorant—not prejudiced.

Somehow, I sensed that the reactions of the board and the dean weren't the true content of their hearts. I don't think the dean believed what he was doing was good, right, and fair. He was given the task of enforcing the board's policy, and he tried to do it the best he knew how. I don't think the board was acting out of spite—but out of fear. They didn't know any better. The board was filled with people from rural areas or small towns where racial equality was seen as a grave threat to their way of life. They were suffering under the pressures of a repressive, racist culture, and they simply didn't know how to reconcile their faith in a gracious, welcoming God with the rampant racism found in all parts of the nation.

I went back to India in 1977, but I couldn't stop thinking about Brenda. Thankfully, pleasant thoughts about me filled her mind and heart. I came back two years later and asked her to marry me. She said, "Yes!" We planned to get married in the church next to the campus where both of us had been very involved. Brenda had tithed faithfully and led the nursing home ministry, among many other ways she had served the church. Before leaving to return to India, I had been the worship leader and choir coordinator, as well as the preacher on occasion when the pastor was away.

Brenda and I made an appointment to see the pastor at the parsonage. When we asked him to marry us, he flatly said, "No." I asked why, and he explained, "Because I don't think your marriage can work. She's white, and you're Indian" (as if we hadn't noticed). I asked if we could rent the church for our wedding. He agreed to my suggestion, and we found another member of the clergy to perform the ceremony.

In this emotionally charged environment, we unwittingly put everyone we invited to the wedding on the horns of a dilemma. Should they come or not? Were they being faithful to their leaders by staying away, or did they have freedom of conscience to come and celebrate with us? Our friends made an array of different choices: some came to the wedding but not the reception, some came to the reception but not the wedding, some came to both, and some didn't come to either one. Our wedding intensified the divisions and suspicions in the Beulah Heights community. For Brenda and me, excruciating pain somewhat clouded our joyous moment.

We had to get away from there. A friend in Oregon had invited me to be his youth pastor. He said, "I can't pay you anything, but I can give you a place to live." Three days after Brenda and I were married, we packed up our car and drove across the country to make a new start.

I served as the church's youth pastor for over a year and then became a pastor in Michigan for about nine years. During that time, our church began supporting Beulah Heights Bible College, and we sent students there. We were happy to help students grow in their faith and learn the skills they'd need for a lifetime of success. The faculty asked me to come back to speak at workshops and symposiums at the school. After many trips back to Atlanta and a lot of time working with faculty, the board gave me an invitation to be a member of the school's board. Suddenly, I was sitting at the same table with those who had passed a policy to prevent me from spending time with Brenda.

To build bridges, I invited several of the board members to come to Michigan to speak at our church. Some of them stayed at our home. In their own way, all of them apologized for how they had treated us. Old wounds were healing. A new understanding was developing. When the president took a role at another university, the board asked me to become the president of Beulah Heights Bible College.

Ten years after Brenda and I left Beulah Heights with deep feelings of hurt and confusion, we returned, but this time, I was the new president of the school. Amazingly, a radical transformation of healing had occurred. The board members now welcomed me as the new leader of the institution.

The darkest chapters of my history occurred at Beulah Heights, but in God's amazing, redemptive grace, He used the same people and the same institution to bring new hope, creativity, and fruitfulness into my life. But first, we needed to clear up a few things. Soon after I took the new role, I went to the dean's office and said, "Years ago I sat in this chair in this office across from you, and you threatened to expel me. I was your janitor. Now I'm your president. I'm okay with you. The question is whether you're okay with me." He assured me that the past was, indeed, past, and we'd move together into the future. In my fifteen years as president of the school, the dean became one of my most trusted and valued partners.

When I arrived as president of Beulah Heights in 1989, we had eighty-seven students; when I left fifteen years later, we had almost eight hundred. When I arrived, we weren't accredited; when I left, we had dual accreditation. No one cheered louder or was more helpful than the dean. His constant refrain was, "Sam, the best is yet to be. We haven't yet seen all that God is going to do here!"

PAIN PARTNERS

Our secrets will kill us. They will haunt our dreams, cloud our plans, and distort our relationships. We may harbor secrets because the truth about a single evil past act or a continuing bad habit is too shameful to tell, or we may keep our secrets hidden because we don't have any real friends who will genuinely listen. Either way, we remain alone, isolated, and desperate to stay hidden.

Kill us? you might object. Surely, it's not that serious. Sometimes it is. When leaders have no place to vent their frustrations and no one to understand their pain, they internalize all the hurt, fear, confusion, and anger. Some experience severe physiological problems that can result in prolonged disease and premature death. And others give up completely. Suicide can become an attractive alternative for leaders who can't see any light in their future. They feel utter isolation and abject hopelessness. When I need gas for my car, I go to a gas station. When I need food, I go to a grocery store or restaurant. Every leader needs to ask: "Who is filling my emotional tank? Who is giving me the sustenance of hope, joy, and understanding?"

Leaders in business, nonprofits, and churches desperately need to find someone who has no agenda except to listen without judging and love without any strings attached. The existential angst of hopelessness and despair can only be addressed in community—close relationships with at least one, preferably a few, who genuinely care for us. Nothing less will do.

Leaders in business, nonprofits, and churches desperately need to find someone who has no agenda except to listen without judging and love without any strings attached.

Almost three out of four pastors say they regularly think of leaving the ministry,[13] many because they don't have a single close friend. Only a few have been loners all their lives. Most of them had wonderful,

---

13 Anugrah Kumar, "Nearly 3 in 4 Pastors Regularly Consider Leaving due to Stress, Study Finds," *Christian Post*, 2014 June 21, www.christianpost.com/news/nearly-3-in-4-pastors-regularly-consider-leaving-due-to-stress-study-finds-121973.

meaningful connections in the past, but something happened: people moved away, the stress of the job sucked the time and life out of one or the other or both, people got too busy and stopped calling and having coffee, a simple misunderstanding grew into an irreparable schism, or betrayal shattered a trusted bond. Whatever the cause, most pastors have no one to lean on, no safety valve, no understanding ear, and no shoulder to cry on.

Pain can only be effectively managed in a trusting, affirming, honest community—not necessarily a large community, but at least a few people who genuinely understand. Most leaders have to endure seasonal storms that last for a while and then subside. For pastors, however, the storms never stop. The torrents keep coming. Without a strong, supportive community, pastors wither away under the pressure. Consider the following questions:

- Who in your life "gets you" and doesn't think you're weak or strange when you wrestle with the complexities of your role?
- Who listens to you without feeling compelled to give you advice?
- Who asks second and third questions to draw you out instead of giving pat answers, simple prescriptions, and easy formulas?
- Who is your safe haven so you can be completely honest and open?
- Who fills your spiritual and emotional gas tank?

The answer to these questions identifies your pain partner—a most cherished friend. In my consulting, I strive to be a safe person with whom people can honestly share their pain.

Stressed-out people are fragile, brittle, and prickly. They aren't usually the most patient people, but keeping friends requires the trait of bearing with people when they are annoying, difficult, and defensive—people just like us! We need wisdom to know when to call a friend on his foolishness and when to let it slide. If it's a recurring problem or one that can cause irreparable harm, we need to step in and speak up and then bear with our friend while he processes what we've said. But more often, we need to let mildly offensive words evaporate in the warmth of our love and understanding. If God nicked us for every foolish, selfish, or offensive thing we thought or said, we'd never have a minute to think about anything else. God bears with us all day, every day. His Spirit very carefully picks the moments to convict us. We should do the same with our friends. A lot of the time, we just need to shut up and be supportive. That's bearing with those who are hurt, brittle, or annoying.

We need to invest our hearts and our time in rebuilding a relationship that has been broken. And if we're friends long enough, misunderstanding and conflict are inevitable. Healing doesn't just happen. In the human body, red blood cells constantly carry nutrients to every part of the body, and when there's a sickness or a wound, the white cells rush the body's healing properties to the site. We invest in the friendship by focusing now on what's good and admirable about our friend—instead of clobbering him in our hearts like we did before we started the healing process. Remember what brought laughter and meaning before the break. Camp out there again, and see if the fires are rekindled.

When we're in pain, the last thing we may want to do is pick up the phone and call someone to ask for help. Everything in us screams, *Hide! Don't be vulnerable! Protect yourself at all costs!* That voice sounds reasonable, but it leads to further isolation, misery, and despair.

When you're in trouble, don't wait. Pick up the phone. Call someone and ask for help. It's essential for your mental and emotional health, and it's necessary for you to be the leader, spouse, and parent you want to be.

When you're in trouble, don't wait. Pick up the phone. Call someone and ask for help. It's essential!

Dr. Sam Chand is a former pastor, college president, and chancellor and now serves as the president emeritus of Beulah Heights University. At Dream Releaser Enterprises, he serves pastors, ministries, governmental and social organizations, and businesses as a leadership architect and change strategist. Sam Chand regularly speaks at leadership conferences, churches, corporations, seminars, and other leadership development venues.

THE 3 LEADERSHIP WARS TO WIN

MRS. NATALIE BORN

High-level leaders understand that there are three leadership wars that must eventually be faced. The first is the war within: how you talk to and lead yourself. The second is the war to see and lead others. Finally, the third is one we all face: the war to win the mission. As we unpack these three wars, it's important to remember that leadership is not linear; leadership styles are always evolving and growing.

Most leaders only focus on the war to win and stay in shallow waters. Standout leaders know they must push off into the deep and give equal priority to all three areas if they are going to reach the mission and calling that God has placed on their lives. Some people are content with taking a black-and-white approach to life, doing what's expected and nothing more. But I believe you are reading this because you know your life has a bigger meaning and purpose; you feel a burning fire inside of you to be more and do more because you know you *are* more.

Leadership doesn't come without land mines, ambushes, and retreats. In this chapter, we will call these out and identify how you can use them to your advantage. Everything in leadership is usable—especially our pains and losses. If we look closely at our battle scars, they can become lessons and allies that eventually lead to victory.

Everything in leadership is usable—especially our pains and losses. If we look closely at our battle scars, they can become lessons and allies that eventually lead to victory.

THE WAR WITHIN: LAND MINES

Several years ago, I found myself in a tough situation at work: my entire department had undergone a restructuring, and I was moved to an unsatisfactory department. I quickly asked a colleague, who was ten years my senior, to meet me for coffee in hopes that he could help me figure out what to do. I felt lost and frustrated and continued asking myself, *How can I cope with losing a dream job and no longer being able to do what I love?*

As we talked through a worksheet by John Maxwell called "The Crucible," my colleague eventually looked up at me and said, "The way I see it, you have two choices: you can either change your attitude or leave." All the blood rushed to my face, and I turned bright red. I sat back in my chair for just a moment, feeling hurt, shocked, and angry. He continued, "You've worked here for many years, and you are about to tarnish your reputation with a bad attitude. It would be better for you to leave with your legacy intact than to destroy your legacy with a bad attitude." I took a deep breath and managed to force out three words I didn't want to admit: "You are right."

One of the most important things we learn when we are leading ourselves is this: when it feels as though we have control over nothing, we still have control over our attitude. It was at that moment, talking with my colleague, that I decided it was time to change my perspective. There were two things I had control over at that moment: my thoughts and my actions. I shifted the focus to asking myself, *What could I build here?*

Those words became critical for me. "What could I build here?" took me from simply being a victim to learning how to create the right scenarios that would lead to victory. "What could I build here?" opened up avenues and possibilities that had not existed days earlier. When our mind is fixated on what was done to us, we shut down the creative part of our brain. When our mind is fixated on what we could build, the possibilities become endless.

Thirty days later, I would march into my executive's office with a plan. I expressed to him that my full talent was not being utilized in this new role and brought data to back up what I believed I should be working on instead. I changed my attitude, took action, and did the work. Joyce Meyer always says, "You can't be pitiful and powerful at the same time." I was done playing the victim. My circumstance had not changed, but how I decided to see it had.

We cannot win the war within if we are fixed on who hurt us and why.

We cannot win the war within if we are fixed on who hurt us and why. We can mourn the loss, but then we must move forward. For so many, a loss takes us out instead of taking us up. The reorganization I experienced happened to me, but all the negative reactions that followed were of my own doing. Self-sabotage is real. Once my coworker helped me see things from a different perspective, I knew that this initially negative situation could result in endless positives. When we want to win the war within, we must:

1) Take every thought captive.

   Second Corinthians 10:5 (NIV) says, "We demolish arguments and every pretension that sets itself up against the knowledge of God, and we take captive every thought to make it obedient to Christ."

   When life and leadership get hard, we cannot allow a stronghold to form in our minds and believe that we have no choices. God's Word gives us perspective and permission to capture negative thoughts that do not align with His Word.

2) Get wise counsel.

   Proverbs 11:14 (NIV) says, "For lack of guidance a nation falls, but victory is won through many advisers."

   When we struggle, we often believe that we must go it alone. Often the enemy wants to single us out and get us alone. But those who are wise surround themselves with people that will speak right into the middle of the mess and help make sense out of chaos.

3) Adopt a growth mindset.

   Isaiah 41:10 (NIV) says, "So do not fear, for I am with you; do not be dismayed, for I am your God. I will strengthen you and help you; I will uphold you with my righteous right hand."

If God is for us, who can be against us? When we are afraid, we start thinking with the limbic part of our brain that focuses on keeping us alive. We instantly think, *Fight, flight*, or *freeze*. That type of thinking shrinks our options. God tells us not to fear. Not fearing enables us to think with the creative part of our brain and expand our options.

After I made the pitch to my executive, he looked at me and said, "I will give you one better." Shortly thereafter, I was partnered with one of our fastest-growing business units in the company. This was a make-or-break moment for my career, and my negative mindset had almost caused me to miss it altogether. In another six months, I was running the entire department. He saw the effort and the attitude, and he decided to trust me with more. The lesson and the message were clear: "Your attitude determines your altitude." The biggest landmine I avoided was my own attitude.

It's Time to Reflect:

- Think about a scenario where your attitude has helped your cause.
- Think about a scenario where your attitude has hurt your cause.
- What was the biggest lesson you learned from the two scenarios?

THE WAR TO SEE OTHERS: AMBUSHES

If you've ever worked in corporate America, you know that it's not for the faint of heart. Competition in the workplace is a constant force in corporate environments. When this competitive nature is utilized in a unified way against external forces, it can help a company succeed, but what happens when competition exists within teams and among peers? When a work environment shifts from competitive to hostile to downright toxic, serious problems emerge. When I joined my new department, Tracy was my peer. I had heard concerns about her leadership style. People frequently complained about her and would roll their eyes when her name was mentioned. Regardless of these opinions, I knew I could have a different experience with her.

After just two weeks into my new role, the situation was getting untenable. Tracy and I couldn't seem to agree on anything. My peers encouraged me to just work around her, but I knew this approach would hurt the company. She was hostile and would often hit below the belt with condescending statements. While I wish I could say that I let her words roll off my back, I didn't. I thought that if I couldn't beat her, I might as well join her. It wasn't long before we could barely be in the same room together.

I felt ambushed, so I called a colleague who knew both of us to help. He told me something I will never forget: "You have to find a common enemy." He was right. I was focused on all the ways we were different and all the reasons we couldn't see eye to eye. What if, instead, I focused outward on something we could both agree on?

When we want to win the war with others, we must:

1) Humble ourselves.

   Philippians 2:3-4 (NIV) says, "Do nothing out of selfish ambition or vain conceit. Rather, in humility value others above yourselves, not looking to your own interests but each of you to the interests of the others."

   We can't build relationships and find common ground if we think we are better than others. Keeping our pride in check when leading is a constant challenge. We have to ask God to help us to see others the way He sees them.

2) Find common ground.

   Matthew 5:43-48 (NIV) says, "'You have heard that it was said, "Love your neighbor and hate your enemy." But I tell you, love your enemies and pray for those who persecute you, that you may be children of your Father in heaven. He causes his sun to rise on the evil and the good, and sends rain on the righteous and the unrighteous. If you love those who love you, what reward will you get? Are not even the tax collectors doing that? And if you greet only your own people, what are you doing more than others? Do not even pagans do that? Be perfect, therefore, as your heavenly Father is perfect.'"

If the rest of the world can love those that love them, where is the testimony in that? Loving those whom others would call unlovable is the mark of a Christ-follower. When we can do that in a work setting, it's powerful. As leaders, we may be the only Christ that people see. We have to carry that understanding with us in all of our interactions.

3) Find a way forward.

Isaiah 30:21 (NIV) says, "Whether you turn to the right or to the left, your ears will hear a voice behind you, saying, 'This is the way; walk in it.'"

One of the hardest things to do is to find a path forward with someone that you don't see eye to eye with. This is where Holy Spirit comes in. He is your guide. He can show you where to go, what to say, and ultimately, what to do.

The day after talking with my colleague, Tracy and I sat down for coffee. I started by asking her for a redo. I explained to her that if we could not collaborate, we would lose this department, including years of effort that she had already invested. The common enemy was the loss we would both face. I asked her a simple question: "Is there anything we can agree on?" Tracy looked up at me and burst into laughter. It was the first time I had seen her look carefree. She leaned in and said, "It's gotten pretty intense, right?" I responded, "Yes, it has. But I think people misinterpret your actions. I think that your frustration and passion come from a place of caring."

If we want to win the war to see and lead others, we must push pride aside and see what people really need.

I walked away from that meeting with an ally. If we want to win *the war to see and lead others*, we must push pride aside and see what people really need. When we read between the lines, we can build bridges with those we would normally consider our enemies. It starts with asking the question behind the question. Behind the anger is a need. Behind the sarcasm is a need. Behind the fear is a need. To see and lead others, we look past their behavior and try our best to surface the real need.

It's Time To Reflect:
- Whom do you find difficult in your life right now?
- What is the common enemy? (Hint: It's about what you're losing by not getting along.)
- Ask God to give you His heart for them. Begin to pray for them, and try to find common ground.

THE WAR TO WIN THE MISSION: RETREATS

I vividly remember the day that God asked me to trust Him with my career. I was sitting in a church service when He began to speak to me. I was working a large corporate job, and, to be quite honest, I was stuck in the grind. I had thought a lot about walking away, but it had always felt like I was retreating or giving up. Letting go of a dream we have built for ourselves and embracing the story that God wants to write in our life can feel terrifying. He invited me to start my own business, followed by a podcast. While I felt scared and unsure of where to begin, I went to my prayer room every day and prayed. Pages of strategy would flow out of those times, and I would use those pages to put everything into motion.

What's your mission? Whether or not it reflects what you're doing right now, what do you ultimately feel called to do? Some people wake up every day to make a living, but I strongly believe it's more important and fulfilling to focus on making a life. That life fills us with mission and purpose. It propels us forward even when things begin to feel impossible.

Some people wake up every day to make a living, but I strongly believe it's more important and fulfilling to focus on making a life.

When we want to win the mission, we must:

1) Know our purpose and our reason for being on this earth.

Proverbs 16:9 (NIV) says, "In their hearts, humans plan their course, but the Lord establishes their steps."

One of my favorite quotes is by Mark Twain. "The two most important days in your life are the day you are born and the day you find out why." If you don't know why you are here on this earth, I would encourage you to stop what you're doing right now and begin to seek God to hear and know your purpose. Your purpose shapes how you lead, what you lead, and where you lead.

2) Know and live by our values.

   Proverbs 2:7 (NIV) says, "He holds success in store for the upright, he is a shield to those whose walk is blameless."

   When we know our values, live by those values, and align them with God's Word, He becomes a shield for us. So often, we are afraid to leap because we are not convinced that the ground underneath us will appear. But when we abide in God, He holds success in store for us. I love that reality!

3) Ask ourselves if we are creating the legacy we want.

   Joshua 4:21-22 (NIV) says, "He said to the Israelites, 'In the future when your descendants ask their parents, "What do these stones mean?" tell them, 'Israel crossed the Jordan on dry ground.'"

   The age-old quote is still powerfully true today: "They may forget what you said, but they will never forget how you made them feel." When we lead, people will look back on our leadership, and the impact will either be positive or negative. People may not remember the work or the project, but they will remember how you made them feel. So what legacy do you want to leave behind?

It's Time To Reflect:

- What is your mission or purpose?
- What do you think it will take to win the mission?
- What do you want your leadership legacy to be?
- Do your mission and who you want to be as a leader align?

BRINGING IT ALL TOGETHER

So, how are you doing? Which war seems to be weighing on you right now? In our leadership experiences, we cannot avoid land mines, ambushes, and retreats. Instead, we must simply learn how to journey through them with peace. As we grow as leaders, we get better at spotting our blind spots over time and begin to understand why they are there. There's nothing like being led by a great leader. Often more is "caught" than "taught" when it comes to leadership. Great leaders are able to inspire the weary, transform failing organizations, and innovate regardless of the internal and external pressures.

The best leaders are able to see around the corners by first dealing with their own shortcomings. We all have them. As we identify them, we have to invite others into our lives to challenge our thinking and hold us accountable. Those that surround us should call us up higher because that's what leadership is all about. No one will follow you because you tell them what to do. They will follow you because you call them to lead at a higher level, provide them with opportunities, and challenge them to take on new heights.

Leadership is not for the faint of heart. But we must overcome ourselves so that we can see, lead others, and win our mission. Now, go ahead, push off into the deep; it will not be easy out there, but the water is just fine.

Mrs. Natalie Born is the founder and chief disruptor of Innovation Meets Leadership and vice president of Innovation for Territory Global. She is a keynote speaker, podcaster, and innovation facilitator. Natalie has worked with organizations such as CareerBuilder, First Data, IHG, and ADPT, in addition to leading major initiatives in over 18 countries.

THE ART OF LEADING CREATIVE PEOPLE

DR. PHIL COOKE

"Innovation distinguishes between a leader and a follower."
—Steve Jobs, Apple co-founder

In many ways, the future of ministry in today's digital age is the ability to lead creative people. No matter how sincere your calling or powerful your gifts, it's difficult to create a social media campaign, record a podcast, produce video, livestream, create television programs, or publish books by yourself. To impact the culture, eventually, you'll need to surround yourself with a team of creative thinkers.

Does that mean you have to be amazingly creative yourself? Not really, but you do need to understand the principles of *leading* creative people, and in the process, it doesn't hurt to sharpen your own creativity as well.

Some time ago, *Business Week* magazine reported:

According to a new survey of 1,500 chief executives conducted by IBM's Institute for Business Value, CEOs identify "creativity"

*as the most important leadership competency for the successful
enterprise of the future.*[14]

Talk to many leaders about the most important leadership competency,
and you'll usually hear about financial expertise, organizational skill, or
motivational ability. But the truth is—especially during this disruptive
digital economy today—creativity is more and more in demand.

If you're a leader, start tapping into your creative side once again.
Management expertise, financial acumen, inspiration, vision—all those
things are important, but to answer the challenges we face today, creativity is becoming more and more valuable (read: critical).

We live in a design-driven culture, where technology is shifting the
traditional rules of doing business and ministry. New times demand
new approaches, and the creative leader will be the one who refuses
to get stuck in old thinking, is willing to challenge the status quo, and
never defends bad ideas with tired lines like, "Well, that's the way we've
always done it."

WHAT YOU SHOULD KNOW ABOUT YOUR TEAM

Whenever I consult with a church, ministry, or nonprofit, I begin by
looking closely at the creative team. Your employees are the ones that
make an organization work, so learning as much as you can about
them matters—and I'm often surprised at how little pastors and other
leaders actually know about the personal side of their team. If you're
not taking the time to know your people well, you're shortchanging
your vision. Having studied teams over the years, here's a starting list
of issues leaders need to know about their teams.

14 Bryan Bourdeau, "Creativity an Essential of an Entrepreneurial Mindset," Courier & Press, 6 Dec.
2010, https://archive.courierpress.com/business/creativity--an-essential-of-an-entrepreneurial-mindset-
ep-445982061-324575931.html/#:~:text=A%20May%202010%20survey%20of,effectiveness%2C%20
influence%20or%20even%20dedication.

Purpose is just as important as talent. Talent is important, and I always recommend hiring the most talented and creative people possible, but start with knowing why your people are there in the first place. Find out who's there just for a paycheck and who's there to change the world. Knowing motivations is crucial for team chemistry and expectations.

Make sure they're in the right seats on the bus. You know the Jim Collins concept—*get the right employees on the bus, make sure they're in the right seats, and then get the wrong ones off the bus.* Brilliantly simple, and yet you'd be amazed at the number of organizations that make serious mistakes in all three areas. The church and ministry worlds abound with employees in positions that conflict with their talents and gifts. That disconnect damages morale because everyone else knows the employee is failing, and everyone else becomes more frustrated by the day.

Know which ones are locked into the rules and which are more flexible. I've worked at organizations that are crippled because employees are so bound by the rules that they can't think outside the box. Rules and policies are important, but you also need a team that knows when to step outside the rules for a bigger purpose. You may remember United Airlines tossing a doctor off the plane in 2017—and the massive public relations disaster that followed—as a sad example of employees who never stopped to think outside the policy.

Finally, of all your tasks as a leader, developing your team is one of the most important. You can't do everything yourself, but when you hand off responsibilities, you need to make sure they're handed to a capable, talented, and motivated employee. Taking the time every day to teach, encourage, and inspire your team will reap more benefits than you can possibly imagine.

And the opposite? If you've been in the ministry long, then you probably know at least one organization that crashed because of a renegade, bitter, angry team and the leaders who let it happen.

WHAT LEADERS GET WRONG WHEN IT COMES TO BUILDING GREAT TEAMS

Building great, creative teams is an art. Like an athletic coach, the key isn't just maximizing the talent of each member; it's also about combining that collective talent to do amazing things. Plenty of sports teams with all-star players lose to less talented teams who know how to work together. But there are five key mistakes I see leaders make over and over that keep them from building a legendary team.

1) **We don't understand what teams are for.** Leaders make decisions, and teams execute decisions. Don't get that confused. I consulted with a large nonprofit once with a leader who was uncomfortable making decisions, so he embraced what he called "team leadership." That meant he had a team of fourteen people who would literally have 8-hour meetings 2-3 times a week to make the smallest, most insignificant decisions. The organization was in chaos—all because the leader was afraid to make decisions himself. I love working with teams, but their greatest strength isn't making decisions; it's executing those decisions. Leaders—don't delegate your authority. Make sure you're using your team for the right thing.

2) **We don't fire enough people.** I love the quote from CEO Jack Welch: "When you don't fire underperforming members of your team, you're not only hurting the organization, you're hurting them—because you're giving them a false sense of what success is." It's not about kicking people to the curb; it's about helping them find the place where they can contribute and grow. Ultimately,

you have to get them out of the job they're failing at right now. And while you're at it—don't confuse "loyalty" and "competence." I love loyalty, but just because an employee is loyal doesn't mean they're actually good at their job.

3) **Our teams are too big.** Numbers can be relative, but once a creative team gets past eight or so people, it doesn't accomplish much because there are just too many opinions. Plus, in a large group, it's too easy for distractions to happen as people start checking emails and having side conversations. I've always liked the advice from Amazon founder Jeff Bezos about the size of effective teams: "If you can't feed your team with two large pizzas in a meeting, you're in trouble."

4) **Finally, team meetings are too long.** I've been in all-day marketing meetings and brainstorming sessions and, after a couple of hours, wanted to pull my hair out. Never forget that people are really good for about forty minutes or so and then need a break. So when it comes to meetings, get creative. Find an interesting location, lower the distraction level, help them focus, create an agenda, and perhaps most important—end on time. When it comes to long meetings, I'll defer to Thomas Sowell: "People who enjoy meetings should not be in charge of anything."

SECRETS TO LEADING HIGH ACHIEVERS

As a leader of people, at some point in your career, you'll have the influence, budget, and resources to build a team of creative high achievers. High achievers come in all packages and personality types and can revolutionize organizations. However, what I find more often is that bosses discover pretty quickly they are way out of their depth when it comes to managing that kind of brilliant, high-energy team—or worse—they become intimidated by their talent. Either way, it's a crisis waiting to happen.

When you get to that point in your career—or if you're already there—here's a handful of good tips for maximizing your leadership ability with high-achieving teams.

Start with yourself. High achievers respect leaders who have high standards, perform well under pressure, and can inspire teams even in the most difficult circumstances. You'll never lead high achievers well if you can't lead yourself.

Treat them differently than low achievers. Far too often (especially in religious or nonprofit organizations), we want to treat everyone the same, but with high achievers, that's a recipe for disaster. Christian principles teach that we respect everyone equally because we are all loved by God equally. However, that doesn't mean our gifts, talents, and skills are equal. When it comes to salaries, office hours, rules, freedom, perks, and other job-related issues, each person on the team should be rewarded based on their value to the project.

Give them the resources they need, and then get out of the way. You're only shooting yourself in the foot when you don't give high achievers the resources they need. Micromanaging is the worst thing you can do with these high performers. So don't let your insecurities as a leader get in the way of allowing them to fly.

Separate them from low achievers. Nothing will drive a high achiever crazy faster than having to work next to a low achiever. My advice? Put them on a different floor, a different room, or better yet—a different building than the other members of your team.

Pay high achievers what they're worth, and stop nit-picking your best people. Sure, working for a "cause" is important, but people have to pay their bills. Obviously, budgets are a challenge for everyone, but when you do have the resources, by holding back financially with your best people, you're killing a big part of their motivation. And if you don't have the budget? Look for other opportunities like time off, a more flexible schedule, etc. Rewards matter.

Finally, give them deadlines, and don't be afraid to add pressure. A dirty little secret among creative people is that *we actually love deadlines*. I even wrote a book on the subject called ***Ideas on a Deadline: How to Be Creative When the Clock is Ticking.*** The worst thing you can do is assign a project and not give your team a date when it's due. Good planning needs benchmarks.

None of these ideas needs to be overdone or cause tension in your organization. But through skillful leadership, you can take your high achievers to even higher levels and, in the process, transform your organization.

DON'T BE AFRAID OF CREATIVE MISFITS

I've always been fascinated with the great artist and inventor Leonardo da Vinci, who, by some accounts, was a brilliant misfit. Some speculate that he may have had Asperger's. At the very least, he didn't socialize well. Reading his biography recently reminded me of a friend who worked for a very large national nonprofit organization. She was remarkably creative, and she showed them how to use digital media in some very innovative ways. She made deals with outside firms to create apps, helped them integrate new platforms to share their message, and created a stable of young filmmakers to produce short films to help share their stories.

While the donors and the public loved the new creativity, the leadership team never got it. They were set in their ways and didn't really understand why she wanted to work late at night or on weekends, challenge their policies, and dress differently than others at the organization.

In spite of the challenges, the results of her work were so successful that she finally asked her boss if she could form an official media department and be the leader. Her frustrated boss told her he'd consider it and set up a meeting to discuss the idea. But when she arrived at the meeting, it was an ambush. Her boss had invited a guest—the head of human resources—who proceeded to read her the riot act about working hours, types of dress, official rules, policies to follow, and much more.

My friend was so discouraged she handed in her resignation the next morning and moved on to another job.

Since that time, the nonprofit has shrunk. Because they didn't understand the value of digital video and social media, they may eventually disappear off the radar. Plus, as their primary group of older donors has aged, they're not being replaced by younger donors—because they don't know how to speak the language of media.

The bottom line is that because they were uncomfortable with a creative misfit, they just might lose their chance at the future. Because they were set in their ways and didn't understand how the culture had changed, they burned the bridge to the next generation.

Creative misfits shake things up. They challenge conventional thinking. They frustrate people. They don't care much about "the way we've always done it."

The lesson? Get comfortable with creative misfits, or get comfortable with struggling to survive.

AN ALTERNATIVE TO HIRING FULL-TIME EMPLOYEES

As churches and ministries grow, most pastors and leaders are convinced they need to hire more full-time employees. Perhaps it's the security of having the team around all the time, maybe it's a loyalty issue, or possibly it's the mistaken idea that to understand the DNA of an organization, you have to be there full-time. Whatever it is, thinking only in terms of full-time employees hurts the organization and can actually hold it back.

The truth is, you can often get far more qualified people by engaging freelancers or consultants than you can by hiring full-time.

Most freelancers and consultants have that job for a reason—they're good enough and have risen to a professional level that multiple organizations want them, so they have the opportunity to impact more than one team.

Plus, in many positions, you don't really need a full-time employee as much as you think. For instance, do you really need a full-time person in areas like:

Graphic design?

Video production?

Video postproduction?

Social media?

Website development?

Writing?

Donor development?

Audio production?

I could go on and on, but you get the picture.

Pastors and leaders—start thinking more in terms of how temporary or part-time employees could bring an entirely new level of expertise to your situation. Why pay full-time benefits and salaries for what could be a short-term creative need?

Freelancers or consultants just might be your answer.

10 VITAL KEYS TO DESIGN A CREATIVE CULTURE

It's no secret that culture is more important than vision. I've worked in creative, vibrant cultures where original thinking is valued, and wonderful things happen. On the other hand, I've worked at organizations where you could literally feel the oppression when you walked into the building. Those destructive cultures often have leaders with great vision and potential, but because the culture is so negative, that vision will never be realized.

How do you create a creative culture? Here are ten principles I've used to turn around numerous organizational cultures:

1) **Creative people need stability.** If they're worried about losing their job, financial problems, or excessive turnover, they'll never release their best ideas. I've seen terrible leaders think they're motivating the team by threatening them with being fired—which is the worst thing you could ever do. Even when you're going through difficult times, create an atmosphere of stability for the team. You'll be rewarded down the road.

2) **Make it safe from excessive criticism.** Critics are a dime a dozen, but creative leaders who can help their team move from bad ideas to legendary ideas are rare. There's a time to look at what doesn't work, but that should be done in an atmosphere of trust. Criticism always goes down better when it comes from a trusted and respected source.

3) **Make sure your leaders are on the same page.** All it takes is one of your leaders to contradict what you're trying to do to wreck a creative culture. At the beginning of building your culture, make absolutely sure your leadership team is unified and moving with you. One critical or disconnected leader or manager can sow seeds of doubt that will topple the entire project.

4) **Be flexible.** Creative people don't all operate on the same schedule or work the same way. Give your team some flexibility, and it will revolutionize their attitude. At one major organization, I talked the CEO into allowing the creative team to rip up carpet, repaint, dump the cubicles, and design their own workspaces. There was fear and trembling on the CEO's part, but within a matter of months, the creative team transformed the ministry.

5) **Get them the tools they need.** Nothing drags a creative team down as much as broken, old, or out-of-date tools. Sure we all have budget challenges, but do whatever you can to get them the right computers, design tools, video equipment—and whatever else they need. Think about it: the less time and energy they spend overcoming technical and equipment problems, the more time and energy they can spend on developing amazing ideas.

6) **Push them outside their comfort zone.** Leaders often think that creative people want to be left alone and operate on their own schedule. Sure they like to create their own timetable, but they also relish a challenge. As I've already said, while they probably won't admit it, creative people love deadlines because it gives them perspective on the project. I don't even start working until I can see the deadline approaching. There is just something about a challenge that gets my blood flowing and the ideas coming.

7) **Get out of their way.** One of the most important aspects of a creative culture, once it's in process, is to get out of the way of your creative team. We all know micromanaging is a disaster for anyone—especially creatives. So give them space, and let them solve problems on their own.

8) **Understand the difference between *organizational* structure and *communication* structure.** This is a huge issue for me. Every organization needs an organizational structure. Who reports to whom matters, and hierarchy is important. But when it comes to communication, I recommend you throw the organizational structure out the window. Your creative team should be able to call anyone to ask questions and discuss ideas. Don't force them to communicate through supervisors, managers, or anyone else. Create a free-flowing communication system, and the ideas will grow.

9) **Walk the factory floor.** Leadership expert John Maxwell recommends that leaders "walk the factory floor" and meet every employee. Develop a personal relationship with employees at all levels—especially when it comes to your creative team. Former Pixar and Disney Animation president Ed Catmull took that seriously—even when it came to giving bonuses. When they produced a box-office success, they would share the profits with the team that produced it—which often numbered more than one hundred people. But Ed didn't just mail or direct deposit the check and send a nice note. Ed took the time to either go to each team member personally or invited them to his office individually and handed them the check—and told them how much their work was appreciated.

10) **Give them credit.** Finally, a great creative culture allows everyone to be noticed for their accomplishments. Never take credit for

your team's work, and always give them the honor that's due. You'll find that when you protect your creative team and allow them to get the glory for their work, they'll follow you into a fire.

Dr. Phil Cooke co-founded Cooke Pictures in 1991 and currently serves as its president. He's produced and directed film and television programming in more than sixty countries and has been influential in shaping the stories of some of the most successful nonprofit and ministry organizations of our time. He's been called the only "working producer in Hollywood with a Ph.D. in Theology."

FOLLOW THE LEADER

STAY CONNECTED

www.ingramcontent.com/pod-product-compliance
Lightning Source LLC
Chambersburg PA
CBHW070543090426
42735CB00013B/3061